No Debt, High Growth, Low Tax

HONG KONG'S ECONOMIC MIRACLE EXPLAINED

No Debt
High Growth
Low Tax

HONG KONG'S ECONOMIC
MIRACLE EXPLAINED

Andrew Purves

SHEPHEARD-WALWYN (PUBLISHERS) LTD
IN ASSOCIATION WITH
THE SCHOOL OF ECONOMIC SCIENCE, LONDON

First published in 2015 by
Shepheard-Walwyn (Publishers) Ltd
107 Parkway House, Sheen Lane,
London SW14 8LS
in association with
The School of Economic Science
11 Mandeville Place
London W1U 3SJ

www.shepheard-walwyn.co.uk
www.ethicaleconomics.org.uk

British Library Cataloguing in Publication Data
A catalogue record of this book
is available from the British Library

ISBN: 978-0-85683-507-0

Typeset by Alacrity, Chesterfield, Sandford, Somerset
Printed and bound in the United Kingdom
by 4edge Limited

Dedicaton

To the people of Cuba, who have suffered for fifty years under a totalitarian ideology which kept them in poverty, but are now poised for great change. All land in Cuba is owned by the state, so by following the leasing arrangement developed in Hong Kong, they could avoid the damaging side effects of absolute private ownership of land. And to my wife and family, who have suffered many years of my arguments in support of radical economic change!

Foreword

Andrew has for many years, held the view that much of the unequal outcome of the capitalist system is due to an inefficient and misdirected system of taxation, which gives a big advantage to property owners, while keeping wages artificially low. This has encouraged him to study economics and the complexities of our tax system.

He became fascinated by the success of Hong Kong (where he spent his early years), and Singapore, and recently visited both Cities to try to better understand the reasons for their success. He also took the opportunity to examine the way that the very successful Hong Kong Mass Transit Railway was funded and explains the process.

I consider this result of his studies to be a well researched and easily read case for the merits of a simple and easily understood tax regime.

I commend his efforts.

SIR WILLIAM PURVES, CBE, DSO, GBM
Group Chairman, HSBC Holdings
1986-1998

Contents

'... without a knowledge of [the law of rent], it is impossible to understand the effect of the progress of wealth on profits and wages, or to trace satisfactorily the influence of taxation on different classes of the community'[1]

'ATHENIAN: There was also another advantage possessed by the men of that day, which greatly lightened the task of passing laws.

'MEGILUS: What advantage?

'ATHENIAN: The legislators of that day, when they equalised property, escaped the great accusation which generally arises in legislation, if a person attempts to disturb the possession of land, or to abolish debts, because he sees that without this reform there can never be any real equality. Now, in general, when the legislator attempts to make a new settlement of such matters, every one meets him with the cry, that "he is not to disturb vested interests"-declaring with imprecations that he is introducing agrarian laws and cancelling of debts, until a man is at his wits end; whereas no one could quarrel with the Dorians for distributing the land – there was nothing to hinder them; and as for debts, they had none which were considerable or of old standing.'[2]

[1] David Ricardo, *On the Principles of Political Economy and Taxation*, 1817, Preface.

[2] Plato, *The Laws*, Book 3, translated by Benjamin Jowett.

I

Introduction

SINCE I was a boy, I have been acutely aware of differences in wealth and opportunity available around the world. Comparing what was available to me, with what I could observe almost from my bedroom window, it seemed obvious that something was wrong with a system that allowed such inequality. That feeling stayed with me as I grew up. Alongside a conventional career in business, I continued to study and ponder this question.

Having been convinced of the efficiency and justice inherent in Land Value Taxation (LVT) in my late twenties, and having begun teaching Economics with Justice[1] some ten years later, the great unanswered question always arose amongst our students: 'Is there somewhere where this is put into practice?'

We continue to struggle to find such a place. The fact is, there are elements of LVT incorporated in several jurisdictions around the world, including the USA, Australia and South Africa, and for a short time LVT was reintroduced as an important form of taxation in Denmark in the 1960s, having first been established in the nineteenth century. Denmark continues to operate a two pronged property tax, with separate valuations for land and improvements (usually buildings). But the fact remains, that there is nowhere where the majority of a nation's public revenue, is raised from the value of land. There is one place however, where a substantial part of public revenue is raised from the land – Hong Kong. The curious thing is, that very few people are aware of it, least of all those people who reside there and live with the consequences. It also has to be said, that the particular form of raising such revenue in Hong Kong is neither a complete system, having

[1] Course taught at School of Economic Science, London (http://www.economicswithjustice.co.uk).

been introduced over the years in an ad hoc manner, nor one which advocates of LVT would recommend. In addition, some of the features and loopholes created by this blind approach in Hong Kong, has in some ways contributed to higher levels of inequality contrary to the predicted outcome.

So, in teaching it has been difficult to use the Hong Kong case as an example. One of the major obstacles has been the lack of evidence and documentation to explain how the revenue is raised. My initial searches, and scouring of text books indicated very little awareness of the unique arrangements pertaining in Hong Kong. Only latterly have I discovered the work of Alice Poon,[1] and a paper by Richard Cullen,[2] both of whom refer to the work of Henry George on LVT in the context of Hong Kong, so I am relieved to discover that I am not alone in my attempt to explain the case.

I grew up in Hong Kong in the '60s, and returned to the island regularly over the following decades, so witnessing at first hand the extraordinary growth of the economy there during the second half of the 20th century. I have taken a keen interest in its history and development since the return to Chinese sovereignty in 1997. It seemed, therefore, that I was well placed, to undertake some research. I am very grateful to my father, who worked there for over thirty years and who made many introductions, as well as to a number of random connections put my way by many people.

This book is an attempt to describe how public revenue is raised in Hong Kong, both through taxation and by other means. The aim is then to compare these methods with those used in the UK, and analyse the main differences.

Before doing so, we need to look at the unique land holding arrangements of Hong Kong, which is the subject of Chapter 2, where I will explore the abstract benefits which accrue to a society organised in this way when it comes to delivering certain public services, particularly transport, and in the case of Hong Kong its underground railway (MTR). In Chapters 3 and 4, I will

---

[1] Alice Poon, *Land and the Ruling Class in Hong Kong*, Enrich Professional Publishing, 2nd edition, 2011.

[2] 'Far East Tax Policy Lessons: Good and Bad Stories from Hong Kong', *Osgoode Hall Law Journal*.

explore taxation, and other forms of raising revenue before returning to a case study of the method of financing the MTR in Hong Kong in Chapter 5.

In Chapter 6, I will look at the situation in Singapore, which bears some resemblance to Hong Kong. I had intended to include a chapter on China, of which Hong Kong is now a Special Administrative Region (SAR), but found it difficult to obtain detailed information in English, so I have added a postscript.

I will not dwell on the logic and merit of the Land Value Tax (LVT), as this has been done by many and various people over the last 150 years, often with great authority and eloquence, for example Henry George,[1] Winston Churchill,[2] and more recently Mark Braund.[3] Sufficient to say, LVT is levied on the value of the site only, ignoring the value of any buildings. Thus the land value is determined by what any willing buyer is prepared to pay for the use of a particular site. It is a market-determined value, based on such factors as natural endowment (soil fertility, presence of minerals etc) and location (proximity to social amenities like transport, schools, parks, hospitals etc). In an urban setting, such as Hong Kong, location is by far the most important determinant of value. It is created by the presence and activity of the surrounding community. The purchaser of a particular plot is putting a price on the benefits conferred by society on that site thereby hoping to recoup his investment. The value of any piece of land will fluctuate as a community grows and prospers or stagnates, and declines.

As these fluctuations are the result of both public investment and the presence of a community rather than the enterprise of the occupant of the site, it is only fair that the benefit should accrue to society, and any decline also be borne by society.

This can be achieved by regularly undertaking a revaluation of all land, and levying an annual charge to the owner in proportion to the resulting value. There would be a separate valuation of any improvements on the site, should the relevant government choose

---

[1] Henry George, *Progress and Poverty*.

[2] Winston Churchill, *The People's Rights*.

[3] Mark Braund, *The Possibility of Progress*.

to raise revenue from the activity undertaken by the owner of the site. The outcome of any business carried out at the site would be down to his or her enterprise, and therefore not necessarily subject to taxation.

The introduction of a full LVT in any economy would give rise to a more just and equitable distribution of wealth in that society. Given that the introduction of a new method of tax will impose new burdens on a number of individuals, it may be necessary to make transitional arrangements for a short period, and it would be essential to cancel or shift the burden from other taxes. At the heart of arguments in favour of LVT is not only that it would create a more level playing field, but that it is economically more efficient, and would allow more real wealth creation. As *The Ecomomist* wrote recently:

> Taxing land and property is one of the most efficient and least distorting ways for governments to raise money. A pure land tax, one without regard to how land is used or what is built on it, is the best sort. Since the amount of land is fixed, taxing it cannot distort supply in the way that taxing work or saving might discourage effort or thrift. Instead, a land tax encourages efficient land use.[1]

The motive for writing this book is to demonstrate the many advantages that have accrued to Hong Kong as a result of raising a substantial part of its public revenue from this land value, a surplus generated by location, or what the Classical Economists termed Economic Rent. Further weight is given to the argument by Adam Smith:

> Both ground-rents and the ordinary rent of land are a species of revenue which the owner, in many cases, enjoys without any care or attention of his own. Though a part of this revenue should be taken from him in order to defray the expenses of the state, no discouragement will thereby be given to any sort of industry. The annual produce of the land and labour of the society, the real wealth of the great body of the people, might be the same after such a tax as before. Ground rents and the ordinary rent of land are, therefore, perhaps, the species of revenue which can best bear to have a peculiar tax upon them.[2]

---

[1] 'Free Exchange/Levying the Land', *The Economist*, June 29th 2013.

Change is always difficult, but the sooner we recognise that most western-style economies have gone down an economically inefficient blind alley of taxation – by collecting public revenue from production and consumption – the sooner our economies will enjoy further real growth. Another benefit may be that manpower might begin to replace machine power in the creation of goods, as labour, shorn of the additional cost of taxation would become more attractive to employers. This might reduce unemployment, as well as reintroducing craftsmanship to the production of ordinary goods, and begin to unwind the massive investment in machines for otherwise quite simple tasks; it may also reduce our reliance on fossil fuels to power the machines.

Opponents will argue that shifting tax in this way (from production and consumption) to land value will only cause firms at the higher value locations to raise their prices to cover the cost of the tax. This is to miss the point on two fronts: first, given that the landlord usually demands the highest possible rent at any particular location, if he is efficient and accurate in his assessment of the rent available, he will not be in a position to increase the rent any further. Second, the activity at each location must be the one which creates the highest surplus value in order to pay the rent, or the LVT due. This is commensurate with achieving the economic efficiency mentioned above. The follow-on effect will be that the lower value locations will pay a lower LVT, or at the margin, no tax at all – thus encouraging more land to come into use at the margin.

Given the regressive nature of taxes on production and consumption (where a higher burden – proportionally – is placed on those with a lower income), such a change may also lead to a reduction in the manifest inequality that surrounds us.

---

[2] Adam Smith, *The Wealth of Nations*, Book 5, Chapter 2.

2

Landholding in Hong Kong

I WILL TAKE as my starting point the date at which Hong Kong became a British territory in 1841, except to note that China, as a nation, has a long tradition of land held under various forms of lease from the Emperor. By contrast, China gave up sovereignty of the island of Hong Kong (and later, in 1860, the piece of land known as the Kowloon peninsula up to what became 'Boundary Street') in perpetuity, by signing the Treaty of Nanjing.[1]

The opium trade with China, carried on under monopoly conditions by the East India Company was an essential part of the triangular trade between Britain, India and China. China, understandably, took exception to the drain of resources – both of its people suffering from the addiction, and its wealth – and periodically raided – or burnt the opium warehouses in Canton (now Ghangzhou). After one such episode, Britain responded, and inflicted a heavy military defeat on China.

Keen to remove their stocks from Chinese territory, in case of future attack the British merchant adventurers in China determined to establish a new trading base on the almost uninhabited island of Hong Kong at the entrance to the Pearl river delta, which formed a perfect deep water harbour giving shelter to their ships at times of tropical storm. Lord Palmerston, Foreign Secretary at the time, described Hong Kong to Queen Victoria as a 'barren rock', but it was not unusual for the government of the

---

[1] The original Convention of Chuenpee ceded the island of Hong Kong only to the UK in January 1841. This was confirmed in August 1842 after consultation with London in the Treaty of Nanjing. In October 1860, the Kowloon peninsula was also ceded to the UK, through the Convention of Beijing, being the land south of Boundary Street. Finally in July 1898 at the second Convention of Beijing, the 99-year lease for the New Territories was signed, including the land of Kowloon north of Boundary Street.

day to play catch up with policy once the agenda had been set by the buccaneers on the front line.

Captain Charles Elliott was the Crown representative faced with the decision about how to accommodate the traders, and their warehouses while dispatches were sent to London to confirm the acceptance of Hong Kong as bounty after the short war. He could not sell land he was not sure would later be owned by the British Government, so decided to auction leases, which could later be converted into freeholds. As it turned out, the British Government liked the idea of the new colony 'paying its way', so stuck with the original plan of granting land for use, under lease, at fixed rents. Having lost the American colonies at the end of the previous century, the British Government was wary of demanding taxes from its colonies, and wisely took the view that local revenue should pay for local services. This logic, in turn, meant that Britain would not be sending money to Hong Kong to pay for the defence of the new colony, thus creating the need for a local revenue source.

Famously, the only piece of freehold land in Hong Kong was given to the Anglican Church, on which now stands St John's Cathedral.

Generally, leases were granted for a total of 75 years, or in some cases 99 years at fixed rents. Later, the majority of the leases on Hong Kong island were converted into 999-year leases, again at fixed rents. This practice was endorsed by the Land Commission Report, which confirmed that the majority of the original 75-year leases in Hong Kong and Kowloon, had been extended to 999-year leases. Examining the logic of conversion, it stated:

> It may be urged that the parties should be kept to the strict performance of their engagements with the Crown, and that where land has risen in value the landlord should be entitled to the unearned increment, at least proportionably with the tenant.
>
> In modern days it has been strenuously urged that the landlord, even if a private individual, has no right to this unearned increment. In case the Crown insists upon its rights, however, the Crown will, at the expiration of 75 years, take not only the unearned increment, but the whole value of the improvements effected by the tenants.

> The Crown in dealing with Crown Lands is not like some private persons selfishly seeking to drive a hard bargain at the expense of the individual, but to dispose of its lands in the best interests of the whole community.[1]

The question, as ever, is what is in the best interests of the whole community. Should the private investor be incentivised to such an extent that the unearned increment remains always in his hands, so that he can continue to invest in industry to create jobs? Or is it in the better interests of the whole community that the unearned increment is socialised, or collected for the public benefit through taxation, year after year? This way, enterprise is rewarded fully, while the unearned increment is available for public investment.

In this instance, the report sided with the private investors, and the Commissioners went on to assert:

> The Commissioners feel sure that the same reasons which decided Earl Grey to sanction the extension of the Town Lots from 75 to 999 years would apply equally to the extension of the Leases of all other lots from 75 to 999 years.

Hong Kong continued to grow as a trading post throughout the nineteenth century, and by the 1890s it was clear more land would be needed to sustain the colony. As a result, a lease was granted by China for a much larger tract of land, including the island of Lantau, known as the New Territories in 1898. This is all the land beyond Boundary Street, running up to the current border between the Hong Kong Special Administrative Region (HKSAR) and China.

The Land Commission, having confirmed the status quo, it might have been assumed this would be how leases in the New Territories would be handled, notwithstanding the fact that the head lease from China was only for 99 years. In the event, the colonial Government, began granting leases for 75 years, some of which were extendable for a further 75 years.

However, it was Joseph Chamberlain, who as Secretary of the Colonies, on 23rd May 1898 wrote to the local Governor:

---

[1] Land Commission Report, 1886-7.

Leases for 999 years are practically equivalent to a freehold tenure and the grant of such leases deprives the Government of all control over the land of the Colony, and of all the advantage of any future enhanced value of the land ..., no further leases for 999 years should be granted, at any rate without previous reference to me in each case.[1]

This was a significant intervention, and it is possible that Chamberlain, as a Liberal member of parliament had been influenced by the ideas of Henry George. It was, after all, the great Liberal reforming administration of Campbell Bannerman in 1906 which attempted to introduce a Land Value Tax in the UK, to which I will refer a little later. Chamberlain, although a Liberal, served with the Unionist Government under Lord Salisbury, and was a noted Imperialist.

By prohibiting any further conversions of 75-year leases to 999 years, Chamberlain bequeathed to the people of Hong Kong a perpetual source of public revenue. It is worth quoting Nissim at length on this topic:

The new instructions from London showed a good appreciation of the benefits of a properly managed leasehold system. They also set the tone for how leaseholds should be treated on expiry of their leases. The author of these instructions could not have possibly conceived of the significance all this would have in the treatment of land under the Sino-British Joint Declaration of 1984, where the precepts of 1898 still hold good.

The reduction of the lease term to 75 years aroused great protest but the only immediate concession that Chamberlain agreed was to make them 75 year leases renewable for one further term.[2]

At the time, there were more Chinese living in the area of the New Territories, particularly farmers serving the needs of the growing population. Various accommodations were reached with them to compensate for the loss of their land, or to ensure they could continue to live within the area of the new lease – and some of those rights continue to exist today.

To jump forward a little in the history, by the early 1970s some

---

[1] Roger Nissim, *Land Administration and Practice in Hong Kong*, Hong Kong University Press, 2nd revised edition, 2008.

[2] *Op. cit.*, Chapter 2, final two paragraphs.

of these leases in the New Territories were due for renewal. Some of the leases were not renewable and new premiums were demanded from those wishing to remain in possession. As for the renewable leases, the question arose as to what to do, as clearly a new lease of 75 years was not possible, given that the head lease was due to revert to China in 1997. China by now was reasserting its position in the hierarchy of nations, and given the ideological differences of the time, the head lease was unlikely to be renewed. Instead, the leases were rolled over by the colonial administration, in return for the payment of an annual 'Crown Rent' enshrined in the Government Leases Ordinance (Cap. 40). As much as anything else, the uncertainty surrounding continued use of land, and the potential disincentive to invest and develop land forced the pace in negotiation with China to agree a way forward beyond 1997. This practice was endorsed by the Joint Declaration between Britain and China in 1984, and has continued up to the present, albeit the Crown Rent became Government Rent on the handover in 1997. Government Rent is currently set at 3% per annum, of the assessed value, such leases being revalued every year. It was also agreed in the joint declaration that non-renewable leases could be extended, without a new premium, but with the application of the same annual rent at 3% of the rateable value.

Thus the Government Rent on leases that had not been renewed, but rolled over, carry a variable charge. This contrasts with the rent charged on the original or longer leases, not yet expired, where the rent remains as fixed at the time of issue of the lease. I will explore the impact of such arrangements later in the chapter.

This accident of history, whereby an arrangement has been made, which in other jurisdictions where land is held under lease would not have been made, is typical of the way practice in relation to land ownership has developed in Hong Kong.

Roger Nissim, who has written the definitive work on land administration in Hong Kong describes the arrangement thus:

> ... what has now been established in Hong Kong is a land tenure system which is, in effect, a perpetual leasehold.[1]

---

[1] *Ibid.*

What this means in practice, is that the Government on the one hand retains ownership of all land – indeed this is written into its Basic Law – while on the other, the user of land is guaranteed continued use of that land, so long as he pays the Government Rent, as well as fulfilling any other obligations imposed from time to time. It also means that the holder of the lease, is able to sell, or assign, the use of that lease to another person or corporation without the trouble of thinking about how long the lease has to run, which in other jurisdictions can detract considerably from the value of the lease.

These arrangements are written into Articles 6 and 7 of the Basic Law. Article 7 reads:

> The land and natural resources within the Hong Kong Special Administrative Region shall be State property. The Government of the Hong Kong Special Administrative Region shall be responsible for their management, use and development and for their lease or grant to individuals, legal persons or organizations for use or development. The revenues derived therefrom shall be exclusively at the disposal of the Government of the Region.

While Article 6 reads:

> The Hong Kong Special Administrative Region shall protect the right of private ownership of property in accordance with law.[1]

This arrangement would appear to give the perfect balance between private and public interest in relation to land. While the government retains ultimate ownership, or 'core proprietary interest'[2] – making it easier to take land back in cases where the public interest dictates – the private user is guaranteed security of tenure with adequate compensation should the need arise for the government to take the land back to serve the interests of the whole community. Readers in the UK will rcognise the difference between the Freeholder and Leaseholder. In the case

---

[1] 'The basic law of the Hong Kong special administrative region of the People's Republic of China', adopted on 4 April 1990 by the Seventh National People's Congress of the People's Republic of China at its Third Session.

[2] A phrase coined by Richard Cullen.

of Hong Kong, there is no separate Freeholder – this function having been retained by the government.

Here, I would like to digress, to examine what gives land its value. When we are buying a piece of land, more often than not, there is a building already existing on that piece of land, and we pay both for the land and the building. The value is determined at the time of sale – when a buyer agrees to pay a specific amount to the seller. They purchase both the land, and the building.

I recall one occasion when selling a house in the UK telling our neighbour who had a three year old boy that we were moving house. The day of the move arrived, and the boy was fascinated to watch as our possessions were gradually loaded into the removal vans. Eventually his patience ran out, as the vans were closed up ready to move, and he demanded to know: 'but when are you moving the house?'

Once the exchange has taken place, the buyer has also purchased the right to use that building sitting on the land. What gives it value to the buyer is the value in use. So while the price may be determined by what an individual can afford to pay at the time of exchange, which might relate to a multiple of his earnings (assuming he has to borrow from a bank to make the purchase) or some other method of valuation at a moment in time, he will continue to derive value in use for as long as he holds that piece of land. He derives value in use whether it is for ten years or a hundred years. As a rule of thumb, land is sold at a price equivalent to the rental value of that property (what someone is prepared to pay in rent) of between ten and thirty years, depending on whether its location attracts a premium, or whether the market is buoyant or not.

However, if he continues to hold that land in perpetuity, it can be said that he derives that value in use forever. So one could say that any particular piece of land has infinite value to the owner. For as long as the land is there, the occupier will derive continued value in use, year after year according to the value placed upon that location by the community surrounding it. As to the building on the piece of land, he will have to invest each year in its maintenance, or if the use to which he wishes to put the location changes, he may need to replace the building.

However, these costs are generally a small fraction of the value in use he can derive from that piece of land. If that were not the case, the building would fall into disrepair, and eventually be abandoned, rather in the way that nomadic communities would move on to a new patch of land, once the fertility on that piece had been exhausted.

Clearly a residential building is providing the owner with the value to her of living there, while a commercial building will provide the opportunity for her business to create wealth by making something, or selling goods or services, according to the best use placed on any particular piece of land derived from its location within a community.

Leasehold property can be sold in the market as easily as freehold, and the property market in Hong Kong is buoyant – operating in the main, just as any other property market operates. In the UK, freeholds generally belong to individuals, companies or government agencies, and are held in perpetuity. Where leases have been created, the freeholder retains the right to charge an annual ground rent (sometimes a peppercorn) depending on the terms of the lease; but when the lease falls due for renewal, if the leaseholder wishes to remain in occupation, he negotiates with the freeholder for an extension of the lease. On prime sites, these lease extensions can run into tens of thousands of pounds. The beneficiary in this case, being the freeholder. If the leaseholder cannot, or chooses not to renew, the land and building reverts in ownership to the freeholder. In the UK, a long leasehold – lets say over a hundred years, generally has the same value as a freehold, even though the terms of ownership are very different; however, where a lease is due to expire even in twenty or thirty years, its value is very much diminished. In Hong Kong, however, where the principle of perpetual leasehold is generally accepted, the value of the lease is not going to diminish over time in the same way.

To illustrate the claim that property is bought at its 'value in use' price, let us look at a few examples of land holding in Hong Kong.

Perhaps the most prestigious address in Hong Kong is 1 Queens Road Central – the headquarters in Hong Kong of the Hong Kong and Shanghai Banking Corporation (HSBC) now one of the world's largest banks by asset value. The headquarters of the bank have been on this site since the bank was established in 1865, although for much of the early years, the Shanghai office was just as, if not more important, than the office in Hong Kong. The bank was founded by Scotsman Sir Thomas Sutherland, and some say HSBC stands for 'Home for Scottish Bank Clerks'. The current Chairman Douglas Flint remains proud of his Scottish heritage. The harbour used to lap against the breakwater running along Queens Road Central, but has long been banished by land reclamation several hundred yards beyond. The building itself has been replaced several times – the one I grew up with was a distinctive layer cake design in a quasi 1930s art deco style, which anyone familiar with the Senate House at the University of London would recognise. The central banking hall was large and imposing with marble steps, pillars and a spectacular mosaic tiled ceiling.

As the bank grew, it was time to redevelop the site to keep pace with technological developments and the computerisation of banking. The dramatic new tower designed by Sir Norman Foster in the 1980s is no less impressive, and it was said at the time, that its revolutionary 'suspended' design with large open floors made it the most expensive office building ever! I have always thought that the reason Banks create imposing buildings is to project permanence and confidence, given the ephemeral nature of the money they create. This building has one startling feature – the ground floor, usually the most valuable space in a retail context has been left open to the elements as a kind of public square or thoroughfare underneath the building, with the entrance being two escalators ascending into the belly of the building, and emerging into an impressive eleven-storey glass and steel atrium, with the teller's counters around the edge. The entire building, therefore seems to float and straddles two plots of adjoining leasehold land. Each plot is more or less the same size: 2,500 square metres, but held under very different terms.

The larger plot on the right, as you face the building with the harbour behind you, is one of the original Marine Lots (No. 104) or ML104 auctioned in the early days of Hong Kong. In 1855, a lease of 999 years for this lot was granted to James Bowman and Francis Bulkely Johnson (of the firm W H Wardley & Co – a company subsequently becoming part of HSBC). I can only presume that this was a conversion of an earlier lease granted for a shorter term. This lease has been assigned a number of times, most recently in 1986 to HSBC itself, for a consideration of HK$6.6bn or £510m. One suspects this was an inter company transaction within the HSBC group. The annual rent, set at the time of the grant of the lease in 1855, is a princely £62 and 10 shillings.

The smaller plot on the left, described as Inland Lot (No. 3566) or IL3566 was granted as a lease of 75 years renewable for 75 years commencing on the first of January 1934 to HSBC. While it changed hands inter-company in 1981 to One Queen's Road Central Ltd, it was assigned again in 1986 for the same consideration as ML104 – HK$6.6bn. After the initial 75-year term (expiring in 2009), one assumes that the lease was rolled over, under the convention described above. The annual rent (adjusted in 2011 under government lease ordinances) has risen somewhat – now HK$ 7,171,664 or £551,666 – this being 3% of the rateable value under the terms associated with Government Rent, although I could not determine what the fixed rent had been for the original lease. Quite a difference, though, from the rent on the adjoining lease ML104, still running at £62 and 10 shillings per annum. In fact the Government Rent in 2011 for IL3566 had fallen a little from that pertaining in 2009 – perhaps reflecting the impact of the global financial crisis still raging at the time.

It is possible, that the valuation (or consideration) given for each lease in 1986 was the same by coincidence, but my experience of surveyors tells me that they do not work in this way. My interpretation is that at the time of the assignment in 1986, each plot held the same value. This was confirmed in 2014, when I asked Roger Nissim, given the different terms, size and length of lease on each plot, what the different values would be. Without hesitation, he said, 'The same'.

This illustrates that the values of each lease are taken to be the values in use, and given the fact that a single building straddles both plots, no one believes that the Hong Kong government is planning to take back the lease in the year 2084, the theoretical date of expiry for the second term of 75 years. Instead, the lease, will be rolled over, and the Government Rent at 3% introduced in 2009, at the expiry of the first 75 years will apply. The rateable value of the whole building in 2013/14 was HK$698.4m.

In fact, under the Basic Law which came into effect in 1997, it was agreed that all leases not already rolled over would be determined after fifty years, in 2047, the length of time that the Basic Law is guaranteed. This would mean that the HSBC lease (IL3566) due to expire in 2084, would expire in 2047, for the Beijing authorities to then decide under what terms the land can continue to be used. However, no one believes that this will happen, on the assumption that the concept of a perpetual lease at 3% will continue.

To take another example, 19 Middle Gap Road, a residential plot with extensive views to the south of the island of Hong Kong, and the South China Sea beyond (also owned by HSBC, perhaps for the use of one of its senior Directors), is Rural Building Lot (No.378) or RBL378. Once again, this lease was for a term of 75 years, renewable for 75 years dated 23/4/1934. It comprises 2,160 square meters, and has on it a somewhat brutalist concrete five-bedroom detached house with generous entertaining space, a swimming pool and gardens. It also changed hands within the HSBC group in 2013 for a consideration of HK$561m (£43m), this time at a very reasonable annual rent of HK$127,548 (£9,811), set at the renewal date of 23/4/2009, the rateable value being HK$4,995,600 (£384,277) in 2013/14. In this case, an increase on that assessed in 2009. Once again, the value in use is demonstrated for a piece of land and a large house with only 70 years remaining on the lease.

One can only imagine the Hong Kong government is satisfied with the income from the Government Rent for the time being. By comparison, in the Royal Borough of Kensington and Chelsea, where the last valuation took place in 1992, the highest Council Tax charged to any property (Band H) is £2133.58 per annum. We will return to a general comparison of taxation between the UK and Hong Kong in Chapter 3.

Now, let us turn to how the Hong Kong government makes land available for use. As we will see, retaining ownership of all land creates some interesting opportunities.

While Hong Kong is one of the most densely populated cities in the world, it has managed to retain quite large areas of green space. Some of this is mountainous, and therefore unsuitable for development, but some areas remain which would be suitable. I often felt that the landscape, particularly when viewed from the sea is very reminiscent of the Scottish highlands and islands, which must have been one reason to make it attractive for the early colonists. Land has also been recycled successfully – most recently the old airport has been re-zoned and brought into new uses, while extensive land has been created through reclamation – both in the harbour area, as well as in ambitious projects in the New Territories, and on Lantau Island. Over 7,700 hectares have been created in this way since 1887 when the first project of land reclamation in Hong Kong harbour was planned.[1] There is evidence of earlier reclamation, but this was probably on an ad hoc basis by the leaseholders of the original coastal lots to make the loading and unloading of their ships easier.

This has given the Hong Kong government the opportunity to make land available – at a price – to its citizens and corporations. It does so through a process of land lease auctions. Today, lists are prepared of new leases to be offered, and one can express an interest, and submit tenders up to the time of the closing date. In the past, lots were offered in open auction rooms, but the process is now more measured. We would call this process a land lease auction, but the people of Hong Kong call this process a land sale. When talking with people in Hong Kong, this led to much confusion on my part, as I did not recognise the sale of a lease as a 'land sale', but in their minds, this is all it is.

To illustrate the process, while I was in Hong Kong, the local newspaper reported on interest in a lease in Ma On Shan,[2] suggesting that eleven bidders had expressed an interest and estimating that bids for the 405,803 square foot (9.3-acre) site were in the range of HK$1.72bn to 3bn. In the event, the site (Sha Tin Town lot 581) was 'sold' for HK$1.82bn (£140m) to Good Assets Ltd, whose parent company Sun Hung Kai Properties is one of

---

[1] Lands Department, Hong Kong Government.

[2] *South China Morning Post*, 22/3/14, 'Ma On Shan site draws keen response'.

the territory's larger developers. What they bought was a 50-year lease or land grant, designated for private residential purposes. The Government Rent for the site will be 3% per annum of the rateable value from time to time, and the development must be completed by end December 2019. The lease also specifies a minimum and maximum gross development area for the site, suggesting that it will be built as low rise town houses. The next phase will be for the developer to submit plans for the development. The site itself lies on a slightly elevated plot on a neck of land overlooking Tolo Harbour, some 300m from the Wu Kai Sha MTR station, which on a good day would take an hour to get you to Central.

In the tax year 2013/14, a total of 41 leases were offered to tender, with two later withdrawn. This represented 338,836 square metres, mostly for residential development, but some commercial space, two petrol stations and one hotel, which raised the highest bid of HK$4.4bn or £338m. No sane person would pay that much for use of a site if they imagined that they would lose the use at the end of the lease term. The same person however, accepts that they will be obliged to pay a Government Rent for that site every year, and the amount paid will vary as the rateable value varies. The rate, as before, will be 3%, whether the land is being used or not.

To take an example of a lease bought by a developer, in this case in the Aberdeen district on the south coast of Hong Kong island at 9 Welfare Road, adjacent to the harbour front: the lot was sold in October 2007, again on a 50-year lease, as Lot No. AIL 451, or Aberdeen Inland Lot 451.

The new lease was agreed on 15/10/2007 for a consideration of HK$5,710m (£439m), again with Government Rent payable at 3% of the rateable value, by the purchaser, Teamer International Ltd. Once the lease had been secured on the land, Teamer International was able to secure finance in return for a mortgage on the property provided by a consortium of banks in the sum of HK$4,655m, which allowed Teamer International to build the flats. Teamer International was perhaps set up to develop the land, and was in turn owned by a consortium comprising K Wah International, Sino Land and the Nan Fung Group. Comprising approximately 6,600 square meters, or

71,000 square feet, six blocks of 37-storey residential apartments have been built, with larger units spread over three floors at ground level with private gardens and a pool. Given that this piece of land was being used in a different way (probably light industrial, or low rise warehousing) at the time of the sale, the process took place under the terms of a lease modification, rather than land sale.

A total of 416 flats have been built, in various configurations, as well as ten Garden House units at ground level, each comprising three floors. There are also some common areas, gardens and Club House facilities. Once the flats are built, the lease is subject to a sub-division into individual lots, each with a share of the original lease, and now liable for their share of the Government Rent, at 3% of the rateable value.

One such subdivision relates to a so-called Garden House Unit 10, a generous four-bed apartment of 2,634 sq ft, including a garden of 699 sq ft and parking space of 600 sq ft, overlooking the Aberdeen Marina. The property reference number being D1986562, with its share of the original Lot 451 being 268/60890, sold for a consideration of HK$167.4m (£12.8m). The rateable value now set (2014/15) at HK$1,606,800 (£123,600), thus making the Government Rent HK$48,204 (£3708) per annum.

A more typical flat, on the 15th floor of block 1, comprising four bedrooms covering a total of 2,000 sq ft, sold on 31/12/12 for HK$53.1m (£4m). The rateable value being HK$836,400, the Government Rent on this property at 3% for the year 2014/15 is HK$25,092 (£1,930). Many of the flats are smaller, perhaps only 1,000 to 1,400 sq ft, and with its views of the Marina and sea beyond, this is clearly a premium development with, one assumes, a good return for the developers.

Forty years ago, Aberdeen harbour was a bustling fishing village (most families living on their boats), with some commercial activities on the shore, including markets, boat repair and a small pleasure boat anchorage. At weekends, we would drive down as a family, leaving the car at the side of the only road, with scrubland on the hills to one side, and a few wooden shacks leading down to the harbour. The click-clack of Mahjong tiles being enthusiastically turned onto the makeshift tables was memorable. We would be ferried to my father's small cruiser by wizened ladies in their sampans, often with a baby strapped to their backs. I don't suppose the inhabitants of these shacks owned the land they were built on – these were shanties thrown up opportunistically to sell cold beers and ropes or bouys to the growing number of boat owners.

I could not imagine at the time how the area would develop. Clearly, it is now a prime site for residential development, and the benefit to the government is illustrated by the transformation which takes place as the needs of the community change. The backdrop for what was once a floating village of fishermen offered a precarious living by the sea is now a picture postcard tableau for aspiring Hong Kong entrepreneurs, who can enjoy a view of green hills, and blue sea stretching to the horizon, while watching their Sunseeker cruiser bobbing in the marina below their balcony!

In normal circumstances of freehold property ownership, when such changes of use occur, the owner of the land at the time of change reaps the full benefit, normally selling out to the developer, who then obtains planning permission for the change of use. The developer hopes to make his own profit from the sale of the new building dreamed up for the site.

In Hong Kong, the government plays a crucial part in this process, working hand in hand with the developer to persuade the owners of any leaseholds on a piece of land to sell at a 'pre-development' price. As a result, the government benefits financially from the premium paid for the lease modification.

In fact, the original legislation passed in 1999 (Land Compulsory Sale for Redevelopment Ordinance) contained a 90% threshold, which was reduced a year later to 80%. Once over 80% of existing leaseholders accept the purchase by the developer, the government steps in to oblige the remaining leaseholders to sell, and then create a new lease, for which the developer is obliged to pay the requisite premium. The rules relating to this process are laid out in the Urban Renewal Authority's Urban Renewal Strategy published in 2011.[1]

The developer usually buys out the existing leaseholders in cash, but can in some cases offer flats in the new development,

---

[1] http://www.ura.org.hk/en/pdf/about/URS_eng_2011.pdf.

often at a corresponding premium, for the improved accommodation. Alice Poon[1] refers to this process in her book, citing it as an example of the cosy link between government and developers in order to maintain a high land price, and keep the profits rolling in for redevelopment of older sites.

This process is again illustrated by examining a new development in the Wanchai district on Hong Kong island. This area, for students of 1960s Suzie Wong style films, was notorious for girly bars and late night brawls whenever naval ships were in town. Originally on the waterfront, gradual reclamation and proximity to Central as well as good transport links have made it attractive for redevelopment. Typically buildings of twenty storeys or less were crammed together in mixed use, some residential some commercial. The surrounding streets were narrow, and often clogged with street markets, with many leases owned either by Sino Land or Hopewell, large Hong Kong developers. Both companies got together to redevelop the area near the Wanchai MTR station, in a series of new buildings called The Avenue. The development comprises four blocks of over forty storeys each, three of them sitting on top of a main podium, with the fourth to one side. The new large urban plot containing the podium is traversed by a pedestrianised 'Avenue', flanked by new shops and restaurants in the style of old Hong Kong, balconied, merchant houses. Until recently these old buildings, festooned with laundry from the upper windows, resonated during the day to the sound of birdsong, with elderly residents taking their caged budgies to the tea houses on the balconies. At night, the more familiar sound was the wail of police sirens, being summoned to the latest fracas outside the bars below. In the surrounding streets forty years ago, open workshops mending cars or welding steel girders competed with wholesalers and cabinet makers for the attention of passing shoppers. Today, these have been replaced with coffee shops, or smart fashion outlets.

With underground parking for residents, most visitors will arrive by MTR – the station is a five minute walk away – or on foot from the local offices. In the upper floors of the podium,

---

[1] Alice Poon, *Land and the Ruling Class in Hong Kong*, Enrich Professional Publishing, 2nd edition, 2011.

there are club house facilities, with open garden areas, a swimming pool, gym, sauna and entertainment spaces, if you want to hold a celebration. This is just as well, as the flats themselves are mostly small (500 sq ft), and yet still command the equivalent of £1m each, and have one bedroom, with an all in one living/dining/kitchen area, and perhaps a small balcony. The view from here is not so grand, as it will most likely be of another balcony to another small flat twenty or so metres distant.

The new lease – Inland Lot 9018 (IL9018) was granted in exchange for the surrender of 36 old leases, to create 1,275 flats for sale to the private sector, as well as shops for rent, a car park and associated public space.

The lease premium was a nominal HK$1,000, but included other special conditions contained in a 274-page document.[1] There is to be situated within the podium of the fourth block, and required as part of the lease terms, a fully fitted facility for an old people's home to be operated by the government or an associated charitable foundation, taking up the first four levels of the building. This is another way in which the government extracts public value from the sale of land, which UK developers will be familiar with in terms of their section 106 agreements with Councils, or the more recent Community Infrastructure Levy (CIL). It is difficult to compare the relative values of premium/lease condition in these two examples, and Poon[2] bemoans the lack of public scrutiny and accountability involved in the lease modification process. Either way, the government continues to benefit, whether directly in cash terms or other infrastructure built. There is also of course the annual income to follow from the 3% Government Rent.

Having covered the process of land sales by auction, or under the terms of a lease modification agreement with the Government's Urban Renewal Authority, we can now turn to a general survey of taxation in Hong Kong, before moving on to other ways that ownership of land has enabled the government to dictate the terms of the development of Hong Kong and its infrastructure.

---

[1] Conditions of Exchange No. 20099, Inland Lot No. 9018, available from the Land Registry in Hong Kong.

[2] *Ibid.*

The prime example of how the government has extracted value from its ownership of land 'by other means' has been in the development of the Mass Transit Railway (MTR) system since 1975. One could say that this process is also a method of raising public revenue in a way that does not prevent or discourage the activity from taking place, as Adam Smith described above (p.4). We will return to this in Chapter 5.

3

Taxation in Hong Kong

STRICTLY speaking, taxation is an arbitrary levy by the government on its people to defray public expenses, and this chapter will compare the methods by which the governments of Hong Kong and the UK undertake this exercise. I am indebted to Michael Littlewood, whose book[1] has outlined much of the background explaining why the system developed for Hong Kong by the British Colonial Administration differs so much from the taxation system operating in the UK, as well as most other Western jurisdictions.

I enjoy the title of Littlewood's book, 'troublingly successful', as I will attempt to explain – but he only hints at the additional forms of public revenue available to the Hong Kong government, as his interpretation of taxation is restricted to the conventional range of arbitrary levies used around the world.

In fact the Hong Kong government follows this convention: when the annual budget is presented to the Legislative Council each year by the Financial Secretary, the figures presented only include the General or Operating Revenue Budget, and excludes the so called Capital Revenue Accounts. Thus, he only reports on the estimates for all conventional tax returns, which I will go into in more detail below. He does not include other forms of public revenue available to the Hong Kong Government.

In essence, Littlewood explains, Hong Kong has generally enjoyed a budget surplus, collecting more in tax than it was willing to spend on public services. Given this fact, whenever it was suggested in the second half of the twentieth century by London, or visiting economists that Hong Kong should adopt a more

---

[1] Michael Littlewood, *Taxation without Representation – the History of Hong Kong's Troublingly Successful Tax System*, Hong Kong University Press, 2010.

normal tax regime, such as a universal pay as you earn (PAYE) income tax (generally paid by the employer) or some form of sales tax such as Value Added Tax (VAT) or General Sales Tax (GST), the Hong Kong administration has appointed a committee to investigate and comment on the proposal under consideration. After a few years, and having 'taken soundings' amongst the local population, including the business elites both Chinese and British, the committee has reported saying the new proposal would not suit Hong Kong conditions. This would in turn be reported to London, and the concept of normalising the tax arrangements in Hong Kong would be forgotten for another decade.

Meanwhile, little mention is made of Hong Kong's other sources of public revenue which help to disguise the true extent of public spending. Don't forget, the incessant introduction of new taxes in most western economies was being driven by the burgeoning welfare state, enhanced after the end of the Second World War, which in some countries consumes up to 50% of their GDP. Two bastions of the advanced countries resisting this tide of public spending were the United States and Hong Kong, where public spending as a percentage of GDP was considered adequate at around 35% and 20% respectively. Since the Financial crisis of 2008, the figure for the USA has crept over 41%, while the figure for Hong Kong is still below 20%.[1]

In the UK, the tax revenue for 2012/13 was £620bn, while expenditure was £717bn[2] with the original income estimate being £592bn. For Hong Kong, the estimate for income in the 2012/13 budget was £27bn.

As a result of Hong Kong's heroic effort to stand against the tide of ever-increasing public spending, many of the world's international organisations engaged in research and comment on Economics often laud the example of Hong Kong, and Hong Kong remains at the top of the Index of Economic Freedom.[3]

---

[1] Government spending as a percentage of GDP: UK 48%, USA 41%, Denmark 57%, Hong Kong 18%. *Index of Economic Freedom 2014*, published by The Heritage Foundation and *The Wall Street Journal*.

[2] National Audit Office, *Whole of Government Accounts 2012/13*.

[3] Published annually by The Heritage Foundation. Hong Kong has been number one for most of the last fifteen years. Singapore has enjoyed the number two spot for a similar length of time.

Milton Friedman, the American Nobel prize winning economist, was fulsome in his praise for the Hong Kong economy, which he considered to be the best example of capitalism at work. He failed, however to point out the basis of the Hong Kong government's prosperity without high taxation: the ownership of all the land. John Cowperthwaite, Hong Kong's Financial Secretary during the period 1961-1971 is also praised for developing a policy of 'positive noninterventionism', which was jealously guarded by many Financial Secretaries and economic commentators who came after him. But he too, did not think it significant to mention the unique form of land holding in Hong Kong. Nor did he or any of his successors suggest any form of liberalisation, or privatisation of the land market.

Before we come to examine some of the unique benefits afforded by public ownership of the land, we set out below a step by step comparison of Hong Kong's taxation with the UK.

Income Tax/Salary Tax
In the UK, Income Tax is deducted at source, and generally paid by the employer under a Pay As You Earn (PAYE) system. Special arrangements exist for those who are self employed, but generally speaking the majority of individuals do not pay Income Tax directly. The first £10,000 of earnings are tax free; earnings between £10,000 and £32,000 are taxed at 20%, while earnings between £32,000 and £150,000 are taxed at 40%, with a top rate of 45% for earnings over £150,000.[1] However, in addition to Income Tax, the employer is also obliged to pay National Insurance. This payment is divided into two classes: employee contributions at 12% of income over a certain threshold (once again, the employer makes the payment on behalf of the employee), and employer contributions at 13.8% of the gross salary paid. Taken together, the effective rate of tax on earnings for those paying the standard rate (20%) is thus boosted by national insurance contributions to 32%, with the employer making an additional payment (13.8% of gross salary) not even seen by the employee. The detail involved in specific tax calculations may make my figures seem inaccurate, but my purpose is not to relate all this

---

[1] All figures and rates quoted here are for the UK tax year 2014/15.

detail, so I apologise in advance for any generalisations, which are made only to illustrate the general state of taxation in each country. One further difference between the UK and Hong Kong: married couples are taxed on their individual earnings in the UK, which gives rise to substantial anomalies for families where either the husband or wife chooses not to work, in order to raise a family.[1] In Hong Kong, married couples are taxed on the household income.

In Hong Kong, tax on earnings is called Salary Tax, and is payable directly by the individual citizen in two installments per annum. The individual is responsible for filing a tax return indicating the different sources of income, as well as their personal circumstances in terms of family and other assets or loans in order to calculate for the various allowances. Crucially, the Hong Kong tax system is schedular, in other words there are separate schedules for each type of income which allows for some types of income to be free of tax altogether. This system was introduced in 1947 under the Inland Revenue Ordinance (IRO). In the UK this kind of schedular system had been more or less abandoned in 1803, but influential business people in Hong Kong were determined to keep different forms (and geographical sources) of income separate. This may have arisen due to the common practice of businesses operating in both China and Hong Kong, two separate jurisdictions, and a desire to retain flexibility in where profits are declared to take advantage of differing tax regimes. This schedular system was reviewed three times, in 1954, 1968 and 1976, by review committees. While the 1976 committee recommended that income tax be assessed on total income as was common in most other countries, the Hong Kong government resisted this reform, and stuck with the schedular system.

Once again, I will take a broad brush approach. Anyone wanting to understand the fine detail is free to research on the HK government's excellent web sites[2], and I have also converted all HK$ amounts to sterling at the rate of HK$13 to the pound, to avoid too many figures. (I have used the same rate throughout the book, for ease of calculation.)

---

[1] See http://www.mothersathomematter.co.uk.

[2] http://www.gov.hk/en/residents/.

There is a similar personal allowance in Hong Kong, giving a tax free income of £9,230, however, if your partner does not earn anything, and you are married, this allowance is doubled. Similarly, there are allowances for children, older dependents (parents) or siblings unable to work who might also be dependent on your income. There is also tax relief on any mortgage interest payments (which were abolished in the UK in 1988), as well as allowances for educational fees you might be paying for your professional development. Taken altogether, these allowances mean that the vast majority of people in Hong Kong pay no Salary Tax.[1]

Turning now to the rates of tax in Hong Kong, the starting rate is 2% on the first £3,076 of taxable income, 7% on the next £3,076, 12% on the next and 17% on the remainder. However, since the financial crisis began in 2008, the Hong Kong government has introduced several waivers, or discounts on the total tax due – currently (2013/14) 75% of the first £770 of tax due has been waived. This waiver is adopted by most low and middle income earners. For those near the top end of the scale, there is an option to adopt a maximum rate (currently 15%) of all 'assessable income' after allowances, rather than adopt the calculation at progressive rates. All citizens can calculate tax due by either method, and then choose to adopt whichever gives the lower figure.

The Hong Kong employee is given a further tax advantage in the sense that Salary Tax is only levied on a strict definition of employment income. Whereas Income Tax in the UK is defined as a tax on all earnings, and special arrangements exist with banks and companies issuing dividends to deduct at source any tax due on interest or dividends. In Hong Kong, there is no tax on interest, dividend income or capital gains realised on the sale of shares or other property (there is one complicated exception to this rule, but I will not go to that level of detail here). In addition, Salary Tax is only levied on income 'arising in or derived from a Hong Kong employment'. One can only imagine the opportunities this presents for creative accountants to create overseas companies or vehicles to process income earned outside the territory!

---

[1] Alan Reynolds, 'Nearly two-thirds of workers pay no income tax', *Washington Post*, July 30 2006.

In the UK, Income Tax raises 26% of all tax revenues, with a further 18% coming from national insurance. In Hong Kong only 14% of general tax revenues come from Salary Tax. In Hong Kong, there is no national insurance.

VAT

Value Added Tax (VAT) is levied in the UK at 20% on all purchases except food (bought in shops where no element of service has been added), books, newspapers, children's clothing and certain forms of educational fees.

There is no VAT or General Sales Tax (GST) on purchases in Hong Kong. However, some commentators, including Richard Cullen and Antonietta Wong[1] argue that there exists a de facto consumption tax on all purchases due to the high price of land – which is passed on in higher rents and higher purchase prices for all consumer goods. This, however is difficult to quantify, and could be said to exist in all major Western cities suffering from high land prices.

In the UK, 17% of all tax revenue is collected through VAT. This is a regressive tax, in the sense that a higher proportion is raised from those on a low income, simply because people on a low income tend to spend all their money every month, whereas those on a higher income can afford to save something in most years. Another feature of the tax in the UK is that most prices in shops are quoted inclusive of the tax, whereas in the USA any sales tax is applied only when the purchase is made – the rates being lower (around 8%) and varying from State to State. A cynic might suggest that the prices in the UK are shown inclusive, in order to hide the true impact of the tax. The large amount of tax collected through VAT in the UK is a major factor ensuring ongoing inequality of income amongst the population.

Customs and Excise Duties

These are the levies raised on various forms of goods sold in the UK, such as cigarettes, alcohol, and petrol. Taken together these duties raised £48bn in 2013/14, another 8% of the tax take. Once again, prices at the point of sale are quoted inclusive of

---

[1] Cullen and Wong, *How History has Shaped the Hong Kong Revenue Regime*, footnote 127.

the duty, thus obscuring the amount of tax being paid on each transaction.

There are no corresponding excise duties levied in Hong Kong.

Corporation Tax

Corporation, or profits tax is the single biggest contributor to the Hong Kong general revenue account at 36% of the total in 2013/14, however, the rate charged to individual companies at 16.5% is low compared to many OECD[1] countries; rates in the UK start at 20%, rising to 23%.

Council Tax, Business Rates and Other Property Taxes

Council Tax and Business Rates in the UK each raise about £26bn for the UK exchequer. Both are flawed in a number of ways. Perhaps because Council Tax is one of the only significant taxes the average British tax payer is aware of paying directly – either by cheque, or more easily by direct debit (so it is not noticed so much) – it is extremely unpopular albeit the tax itself is not excessive. For this reason, the rates of the tax have not been changed since the introduction of the tax in 1992. The Council Tax replaced the infamous Poll Tax, which was again levied directly but on each individual over 18 living at an address, rather than on the property itself.

The experimental introduction of the Poll Tax in Scotland is considered to have caused the collapse of the Conservative Party in Scotland, and remains a significant factor in the resentment felt towards England, which manifested in the debate on Independence for Scotland in 2014. When the Poll Tax was introduced in England, riots in the street ensued, and the imposition of this very obvious tax is generally considered to have contributed to the resignation of Margaret Thatcher as Prime Minister in 1991. All this drama surrounding a relatively small tax, compared to larger impositions such as income tax, only demonstrates the danger of a government being too overt in the method of taxation. Best to keep taxes hidden from the individual you are taxing.

---

[1] Organisation for Economic Co-operation and Development, comprising 32 of the largest Western economies.

Meanwhile UK property prices have increased significantly, but the charging bands of property values have not kept pace. For advocates of a tax on land values, the major issue with Council Tax is that it based on the combined value of the land and any building, rather than on the land value alone.

By contrast the Business Rates have been assessed more recently (2010). They are usually assessed every five years, but the Coalition Government in the UK has delayed the 2015 assessment until 2017. This has proved unpopular, given that many commercial rents for new leases have fallen since the last assessment in 2010, and yet the Business Rates have not reflected this fall. Once again, the assessment is raised on the building alone – and if there is no building on the land, no tax is due. Until recently, if a building was empty or considered unfit for use (for example with no running water) there was no tax to pay, but with this exemption restricted to six months, many landowners with redundant buildings, have responded by simply demolishing the building, rather than pay the tax. One redeeming feature of the Business Rate is that it redistributes the tax collected from Councils with high value locations to Councils with lower value locations, thus recognising in part the different locational values of land.

In Hong Kong, other than Government Rent assessed at 3% of the rateable value (on qualifying leases), property is taxed in a number of additional ways. The General Rates are paid by occupiers of all rateable premises, raising 4% of the total revenue. It is levied on all owners of land and/or buildings, at the standard rate of 16% of rateable value per annum. It is worth noting, that in Hong Kong, property taxes are paid by the owner, not the tenant of a building as in the UK. If the tenant is asked to pay as a matter of convenience, he can deduct the amount paid in property tax from his rent. Many people would argue that if property taxes were levied on the owner of a building, where currently the tenant pays the tax, she would pass it on to the tenant by means of a higher rent. However, given that landlords should be operating according to the tenets of the free market – whereby she is already charging the highest possible rent – it gives her no scope to pass on any new tax, such as LVT.

The General Rates are not to be confused with the tax on property rental income, which the owner of property in Hong

Kong also pays: Tax on rental income derived from Hong Kong properties is charged at a flat rate of 15% on 80% of the actual rental income received during any given tax year. This is called the net assessable value, and once again is paid by the owner, not the tenant.

So there are in fact three taxes paid by the owner: the Government Rent at 3% of rateable value; the General Rates at 16% of rateable value; the tax on rental income at 15% of 80% of actual income received.

Also included in the General Revenue account for Hong Kong are income generated by Government land licences and rents (other than Government Rent assessed at 3% of the rateable value). These may be short term licences or rents for ad hoc government owned property, rents from government quarters (due from employees) as well as other rents from government properties, constituting a relatively paltry HK$4.3bn or £330m in 2011/12.

Government Rent itself raised HK$6.4bn (£492m) in 2011/12, rising to HK$7.8bn (£600m) in 2012/13. It has steadily increased over the last twenty years, raising a mere HK$3.1bn (£238m) in 1997/98. Another feature of Government Rent is that, given the rateable values are assessed each year, in times of recession the rent will fall, as indeed happened in 2004/05 immediately after the SARS[1] epidemic. Over the next few decades this figure is likely to rise, as more land sales (lease auctions) are undertaken on a variable rental basis – Nissim's perpetual lease arrangement – and as existing leases fall due for renewal, or roll over at the new variable Government Rent as has happened up to now.

During the research into Government Rent, I felt that the amount raised by this method was rather low; so, in order to get a feel for how many Leases were paying Government Rent at the 3% variable rate, I asked the Land Department how many leases of different lengths existed. They could not tell me. Although there is an electronic record of each lease granted, some copied from the original paper, so called Memorial deeds, and although one can examine all leases by an interactive Geodetic online map

---

[1] Severe Acute Respiratory Syndrome, a virus that affected the Hong Kong population in the previous year.

– there is no central record of the number of each type of lease, and when they fall due for renewal. It is not clear how the department calls in leases for renewal, or a change in rental terms, but assuming there will be a steady stream of 75+75-year leases coming up in the next fifty years, I would expect the income from Government Rent to increase substantially over the coming years.

Stamp Duty is a form of transactional property tax used in both jurisdictions. Indeed, the UK government rebranded the Stamp Duty on immovable property as the Stamp Duty Land Tax (SDLT), in order to distinguish it from stamp duties on the sale of equities.

The UK government has tinkered with the rates payable somewhat over recent years – in some cases to incentivise first time buyers. However, a surprise wholesale reform was announced in the 2014 Autumn Statement. Rates now vary from zero, for properties up to £125k (HK$1.6m) in value to 12% for properties worth more than £1.5m (HK$19.5m), with the percentage rate applying to the portion of the price within each band (December 2014).

In recognition of various loopholes in this regime, whereby companies were being created to buy residential properties, the UK government introduced a 15% charge for such transactions worth over £500k in 2014. Previously, the company owning the residential property could be sold, rather than the property thus reducing the tax liability on exchange. In addition, an Annual Tax on Enveloped Dwellings (ATED) was introduced in the same year for residential properties owned by companies with a value of more than £2m. The charge starts at £15,400 per annum for properties worth more than £2m, rising to an annual charge of £143,750 on properties worth more than £20m. While these arrangements apply to a small niche in the market, they are nonetheless welcome developments in government thinking towards property ownership, and the damage which can be caused by a property market dominated by the idea of a house being considered as an investment, rather than as somewhere to live.

The UK revenue from Stamp Duty in 2012/13 was £9.1bn – £2.2bn coming from the tax on share transactions, and £6.9bn coming from SDLT. As a percentage of the total revenue, however, Stamp Duty is not significant.

The Hong Kong government has taken creativity with Stamp Duty to a new level in an attempt to reduce property speculation and take the heat out of one of the most expensive property markets in the world. The rates on standard Ad Valorem Stamp Duty (AVD) in Hong Kong start at 1.5%, rising to 8.5% for properties over HK$21.7m (£1.6m). AVD is payable by the seller of the property whereas in the UK, it is paid by the buyer.

In 2014, the Hong Kong government introduced a Special Stamp Duty (SSD) for any properties bought after November 2010, with higher rates for properties bought after October 2012, whereby if the property is sold within two years of purchase, the special rate of 10% applies – rising to 20% if the property is held for less than 6 months. Once again SSD is paid by the seller. Also since October 2012, a Buyers Stamp Duty (BSD) is charged at the flat rate of 15% on the value of the property, payable by the buyer, although this only applies to buyers who are not permanent residents of Hong Kong. In addition, Double Stamp Duty (DSD) at higher rates, has been applied to the AVD again, only for foreign buyers, and buyers of second properties; these latter policies have clearly deterred buyers from Mainland China and speculators, with a consequent cooling of the Hong Kong property market.

Despite this cooling, the Hong Kong government stands to increase the return from its various forms of Stamp Duty substantially. The revenue in 2011/12 was HK$44bn (£3.3bn), or 12% of the total.

Betting Tax

Both countries raise revenue from betting. In the UK, the amount is not significant, but in Hong Kong, the revenue from betting at HK$15.7bn or £1.2bn is 5% of the total. There is another feature of the betting market in Hong Kong, which has further benefits (if you can say that betting ever has any benefit to the individual!) which is that all betting is conducted by the Hong Kong Jockey Club, a not for profit company, which holds a monopoly on all betting in Hong Kong.

The first horse race took place in Hong Kong in 1845. The British love to race, the Chinese love to gamble. In 1884 the Royal Hong Kong Jockey Club was established, and in 1955 the not for profit Club decided to allocate all its surplus to various charities in response to the growing tide of refugees from China arriving in Hong Kong to escape the revolution there. Soon after, the government granted the club the only licence to manage all gambling in the territory, which now includes a lottery and betting on football results worldwide. So in addition to the 5% contribution from the betting tax, making the club the largest taxpayer in Hong Kong, the renamed (after 1997) Hong Kong Jockey Club gave £133m to charities in Hong Kong in the year 2011/12, catering in particular for the elderly and disabled. In fact, many capital projects in Hong Kong, including schools and hospitals, as well as the rebuilt Government Stadium have been paid for directly by the Jockey Club, in addition to the tax they pay, and their donations to charities. They also pay for all the administrative costs of the so called Community Chest (a Hong Kong charity), which distributed a further £17m to various projects last year.

Indeed, the mission statement of the Hong Kong Jockey Club is:

> To be a world leader in the provision of horse racing, sporting and betting entertainment, and Hong Kong's premier charity and community benefactor.[1]

Would William Hill (a UK betting company operating in nine countries with 17,000 employees) or the owners of Ascot racecourse (one of the UK's most prestigious racing venues) ever adopt such a mission statement, whilst providing a similar level of entertainment and customer satisfaction? For the record, William Hill's website states:

> At William Hill, we focus on continuing to create value for our investors by drawing on our core capabilities and strengths in sports betting and cross-sell into gaming.[2]

Is this another happy accident for the people of Hong Kong, or the work of an enlightened (if perhaps out of character) colonial administrator? We can also speculate as to whether a betting tax satisfies Adam Smith's suggestion that an economically

---

[1] http://www.hkjc.com/home/english/.

[2] http://www.williamhillplc.com/investors.aspx.

efficient tax should leave the activity at the same level after the tax as it was before the tax.

Utilities, Fees & Charges

We are now coming to the fag end of measures to raise revenue in each country, that category which is usually referred to in the accounts as 'other'. The individual amounts in each category are relatively small, but taken together, in the UK, 'other' taxes raise 14% of the total, while in Hong Kong the amount is 17% of the total. I do not intend to go into detail in these two areas, which in the UK includes such things as Air Passenger Duty, and Insurance Premium Tax.

However, in Hong Kong there is a category entitled Utilities, Fees & Charges, which does not feature separately in the UK – the Hong Kong government raised 5% of their revenue in 2012/13 from such things as new car registrations, and motor boat licences among other, usually discretionary forms of expenditure undertaken by the better off. It was also one of Adam Smith's recommendations that those who wish to benefit from the use of something should pay for the privilege, which in some way justifies this category. While in the UK, no doubt some similar charges raise additional revenue, it is not as significant as it is in Hong Kong.

Estate Duty

Although these raise an insignificant amount in the UK, there is no Estate Duty (Inheritance Tax) in Hong Kong, having been abolished over a decade ago. Nonetheless it is a significant annoyance to those affected in the UK, once again because the beneficiaries of the Estate become aware of how much they are forgoing when the time comes. The Conservative Party in the UK gave a considerable boost to their fortunes in 2007 when they announced a proposal to raise the inheritance tax threshold from £325k to £1m; however, since being in government this particular policy has not seen the light of day! As the election of 2015 approaches, it was no surprise for hints to be dropped at the Conservative Party conference in September 2014, that the £1m threshold would once again be on the agenda for the manifesto. Many people object to inheritance tax on the basis that it represents a double taxation – taxing income that has already been taxed. From a Georgist point of view, inheritance tax is merely the method by which the government claws back a portion of the value in land (created by the community) which has not been collected during the individual's lifetime; so one could say there is some justice in this form of taxation.

Investment Income

There is a peculiar entry in the list of Hong Kong government revenue, Investment Income, which does not appear in the UK listing. HK$26.3bn (£2bn) makes up 7% of all revenue, and includes investment income and interest, as well as returns on equity investments in statutory agencies and corporations. I suspect there is some such income in the UK government accounts, but it is likely to be insignificant. In fact, whenever a UK government agency such as the Land Registry becomes too adept at generating profit from fees, the UK government is likely to propose a privatisation, in order to enjoy a one off gain. After a vigorous public campaign, the Land Registry in the UK was in fact given a reprieve in 2014, and remains in public ownership.

One cannot describe this investment income as taxation, as it is not an arbitrary levy on the population at large; however it is included in the HKSAR general revenue account, and therefore I have included it at the end of this chapter, as it highlights the contrasting fortunes for the UK Exchequer. There is no entry in the UK accounts of Public Revenue for investment income. Quite the contrary, in the UK, under the list of government spending, there is an entry – Interest on Government Debt – nearly £49bn, or 7% of total spending in 2011/12.[1] Hong Kong has no corresponding entry in their list of government spending, although some of the departments involved with infrastructure investment have issued bonds to the public, on which interest is paid. However, this is accounted for in the records for individual funds.

I will return to this topic, and the source of this investment income for the Hong Kong government in the next chapter, but for now we can conclude this comparison of the conventional taxation methods in Hong Kong and the UK. One general statement

[1] Office for National Statistics.

that can be made, is that the method of taxation is much simpler in Hong Kong than it is in the UK. It is also more transparent, in the sense that each individual citizen pays the tax directly to the government every quarter. There is no agent collecting the tax on behalf of the government, such as the employer (in the case of PAYE and National Insurance) or the retailer (in the case of VAT) as is the case in the UK. Perhaps this explains why the general level of taxation in Hong Kong is so much lower than it is in the UK. The population is more aware of how much tax is being paid, and therefore more vigilant in raising opposition when a new tax is proposed, or rates are raised.

4

Other Sources of Revenue in Hong Kong

W E NOW turn to the other sources of public revenue the government enjoys in Hong Kong, which don't feature in the UK. Strictly speaking, these are not taxes, but nevertheless contribute significantly to the wellbeing of the people of Hong Kong.

Listed in the Annual Report of the HKSAR, in addition to the General Revenue Account are a series of reports on Funds with specific purposes, their own constitutions and areas of responsibility for investment and expenditure. They are all listed on the Hong Kong Treasury web site, as part of the annual accounts[1] and anyone interested in the fine detail could spend a few days examining them further. The list consists of:

Capital Works Reserve Fund
Capital Investment Fund
Civil Service Pension Reserve Fund
Disaster Relief Fund
Innovation and Technology Fund
Land Fund
Loan Fund
Lotteries Fund
Bond Fund

Some funds are larger than others, and some are active, while others are passive.

You will recall that the HKSAR Basic Law states that all land in the territory is owned by the government, and that through the mechanism of lease ownership it comes to be used by private companies and individuals.

---

[1] http://www.try.gov.hk/internet/eharch_annu_statend13.html#p.

Land Sales

Therefore, it should come as no surprise that the biggest source of annual income from property in Hong Kong relates to the sale of new leases. These are the so called Land Sales for new leases on land released for development, or reclaimed from the sea, as well as new leases for land consolidated by the Urban Renewal Authority. We discussed the mechanics of these arrangements in Chapter 2. Receipts from these lease auctions are the main reason Hong Kong consistently accumulates surplus funds. This income is not included in the annual budgeting process reported in the General Revenue Account, instead being accounted for in the Capital Works Reserve Fund annual report.

All these Funds are managed by the Hong Kong Monetary Authority, together with the Exchange Fund, – which is used to manage the pegging of the HK$ to the US$ at one US$ to 7.80 HK$ since 1983 – which was designed to bring monetary stability to the Hong Kong market which was so dependent on the export of manufactured goods including textiles and electricals at the time.

Capital Works Reserve Fund

In the year 2012/13, £5.3bn was collected in Land Premiums. The result of tenders published by the Land Department gives a slightly different figure, but I will use the figure in the published accounts of the Capital Works Reserve Fund here. This includes premiums in respect of lease modifications and exchanges or extensions, for example, for change of use, which produced income of HK$24.3bn (£1.8bn). In addition to land premiums the Capital Works Reserve Fund has its own investment income – £346m (from deposits with the Exchange Fund) as well as assorted other income, providing a total income in the year 2012/13 of HK$74.2bn (£5.7bn).

A total amount of HK$66.5bn (£5.1bn) was spent through the same fund on infrastructure projects including roads, buildings, ports, housing and airports, not counted as part of the annual current account expenditure. This helps explain why public spending in Hong Kong seems to be so much lower than in the UK. This spending added 16% to overall expenditure. If this income were included in the current account revenue, it would significantly increase the proportion of revenue collected from ownership, or control of property leases.

The retained earnings, or balance in the Capital Works Reserve Fund, HK$77.9bn (£5.9bn), is invested in the Exchange Fund.

Land Fund

Some Funds are more active than others. For example, the Land Fund, established on 1st July 1997 (the handover of Hong Kong to China) with the balance of the Colonial Government Land Fund, seems only to be a vehicle for investment. Its assets are managed by the Exchange Fund, and at the year end March 2013 totalled HK$209bn (£16bn) after recording income of HK$11bn (£846m) for the year. Over the years, there have been transfers to and from the General Account, but the total assets have been more or less stable since its inception.

Capital Investment Fund

The Capital Investment Fund established in 1990, for the purpose of financing the ongoing development of MTR, is a bit of a hybrid, being the holding vehicle for government equity positions in a host of public assets including the Hong Kong Housing Authority, Kowloon to Canton Railway Corporation, Science and Technology Parks, Asian Development Bank, the Airport Authority, the International Exhibition Centre and the Urban Renewal Authority amongst others. The total assets held in the fund amounted at end March 2013 to HK$547bn (£42bn). Annual movement in this fund is relatively low, as it is primarily a holding account for the assets of the Hong Kong Government.

Hong Kong Monetary Authority

The other smaller funds, each with a particular remit, added only £200m to public spending in 2012/13. However, having opened the Pandora's box of funds, it is opportune to discuss the Hong Kong Monetary Authority (HKMA). Its key functions are to guarantee monetary and banking stability, much in the way the Bank of England functions in the UK, as well as promoting Hong Kong as an international financial centre, a job undertaken in the UK by the Corporation of London, and the Lord Mayor (not to be confused with the Mayor of London, who has more traditional responsibilities for London wide infrastructure). In addition, the HKMA manages the Exchange Fund, an amalgamation of all the individual Funds detailed above. It also performs the role of lender of last resort, or Central Bank, like the Bank of England. Until the creation in 1983 of the HKMA, the Hong Kong Bank (now HSBC) carried out this function, which was the source of much envy from other financial firms before the HKMA was established. This is Hong Kong's Sovereign Wealth Fund (SWF). As well as providing finance for all sorts of Public Works, it is the source of the Investment Income in the General Revenue Account.

Some argue that the HKMA is not a Sovereign Wealth Fund, and the HKMA does not describe itself as one. However, given the fact that they are listed as the eighth largest fund in the world by the Sovereign Wealth Fund Institute, and part of their activity involves managing the Exchange Fund which generates invest-ment income for the HKSAR, I think it is legitimate to consider it as an SWF, albeit with other roles incorporated into its govern-ing document. Perhaps we can take 1998, when the assets of the Land Fund were transferred to the Exchange Fund, as the starting point for the transformation of the HKMA from a simple monetary authority into an SWF.

The HKMA's primary role 'is to affect, either directly or indirectly, the exchange value of the currency of Hong Kong'.[1] At the end of 2013, the Exchange Fund's assets amounted to HK$3,032.8bn (£233.3bn) – not bad for a barren rock in the South China Sea – with investment income of HK$81.2bn (£6.2bn) in that year, some of which is retained in the Exchange Fund, while other tranches are returned to the General Revenue Account as is the case with the individual Funds mentioned above. The value of the Exchange Fund amounts to 142% of annual GDP. If Hong Kong were a company, it would be like saying that the company had a reserve worth more than its annual turnover. This would be a very successful company, and if it were a private company, there would be demands from shareholders for special dividends!

By contrast, the UK government has no Sovereign Wealth Fund. Just the opposite, by the end of July 2013, 'public sector net debt excluding temporary effects of financial interventions

---

[1] http://www.hkma.gov.hk/eng/key-functions/exchange-fund.shtml.

(PSND ex) was £1,193.4 billion (HK$15,514.2bn), equivalent to 74.5% of gross domestic product'.[1]

Could the method of land ownership, or the conditions under which land can be used by individuals and companies in Hong Kong have something to do with the contrasting fortunes of the UK and Hong Kong? Could this also explain the low rates of personal income tax in Hong Kong, in contrast to almost every other western economy? Is this the hidden answer to Littlewood's 'troublingly successful' tax system? I will return to this question in the chapter on Singapore.

Before going on to examine the Hong Kong method of raising public revenue against the theory advocated by supporters of LVT, it is useful to give just a few more broad brush figures comparing the fortunes of the two economies.

Economy comparisons	UK	HK
Gross Domestic Product £bn 2012/13	1,525.0	163.2
Population – million	63	7.15
GDP growth ten-year average %	2.3	4.5
GDP per capita 2012 £	24,118	22,997
Unemployment % of working population	7.4	3.3
CPI inflation 2013 %	2.1	4.3
Public expenditure as % of GDP	44.7	19.0
Official reserves/Fiscal reserves 2013 £bn	31	56
Owner occupiers % 2011/13	64	56
Public expenditure per capita £	10,825	4,303

UK figures have been taken from various sources available from the Office of National Statistics. The Hong Kong figures have been taken from the 2014 edition of *Hong Kong in Figures*, published by the HKSAR Government. In most cases, they have remained consistent over several years. The quoted public expenditure as a percentage of GDP excludes the spending highlighted above, undertaken outside of the General Revenue Account. All figures have been converted to sterling at HK$13 to the pound.

---

[1] http://www.ons.gov.uk/ons/rel/psa/public-sector-finances/july-2013/stb—july-2013.html#tab-Latest-figures.

Following on from this summary, what services does the HKSAR provide, either directly or indirectly to its citizens?

I do not intend to slavishly compare and contrast the levels of government spending between the UK and Hong Kong. Most readers in the UK will have a general idea of what is available in the UK, and readers in other countries will have an idea for their own domicile. I will give some general comparisons for readers in Hong Kong, in order to guage the generosity of their own government.

Education

The HKSAR has provided, since 2008/09 twelve years of free education – six years primary, from ages 6 to 12, and six years secondary, which may include vocational training for those inclined to more practical skills. Nursery education is offered to children age 3 to 6 by private institutions or voluntary bodies; however, these schools are heavily subsidised by way of voucher schemes for parents, rent/rate rebates or free accommodation in public housing estates. There are 28 institutions offering self financed post secondary education, as well as 17 degree-awarding higher education institutions. Nine of these are Universities awarding degrees, of which seven are supported by the Hong Kong University Grants Committee. Loans are available for qualifying students, as well as tax allowances for working people wishing to study for further qualifications.

In the UK there is very little, if any, subsidised pre-school education, while a voucher scheme lasted only two or three years in the early nineties. Free primary education starts at age 5, and pupils transition into secondary education at age 11, and can continue either in school or vocational college up to age 18. University or vocational college education is available to qualifying students with a loan scheme to pay both fees and living expenses which is means tested.

Hong Kong is a highly developed service economy with a good percentage of its population holding tertiary qualifications – 21% with degrees, and a further 8% with post secondary qualifications. It enjoys low levels of unemployment, and shook off the effects of the recent financial crisis with ease, with over 50% of the population working in the service sector, classified as white collar work.

Housing

It is perhaps surprising to learn that while in Hong Kong over 50% of the population are owner occupiers, 30% are in public rental housing (PRH) with the balance in various forms of subsidised private homes, or private rented accommodation. To break this down further: as of March 2012, there were about 1.4m private residential housing units and 766,300 PRH units. Since 1978, 467,800 subsidised flats had been sold at discounted prices to the occupant under the Home Ownership Scheme (HOS) among others. Of these, 75,100 flats could be traded on the open market after payment of a premium, and in some cases a nil premium applied, should the new owner wish to sell the flat.[1] While the HOS scheme was suspended in 2003, it resumed in 2011, with an ambition to build an annual average of 5,000 units. Access to PRH units is means tested, under a points scheme depending on both income and length of time resident in Hong Kong. PRH units do not pass from one generation to another automatically, and if tenants begin to earn more, they have to pay more rent, or vacate their flats. Families who own property elsewhere in Hong Kong, cease to be eligible for PRH accommodation. Monthly rents for PRH units, inclusive of rates and management fees as well as maintenance costs, range from HK$290 (£22.30) to $3,880 (£298), while the average rent is HK$1540 (£118).

The ongoing investment in PRH units is confusing. The stated ambition of the Housing Authority is to build 5,000 units per annum. According to the Capital Works Reserve Fund estimates, only HK$609m (£47m) was to be spent on 'Housing' in 2013/14, but a further HK$3.5bn (£269m) was to be spent on land acquisition, and HK$7.8bn (£600m) on 'buildings'. According to the Budget of the Hong Kong Housing Authority on the other hand, the total capital expenditure is expected to be HK$11.9bn (£915m) in 2013/14, with the vast majority of that to be spent on construction costs.[2] Adding together the figures from the Capital Works Reserve Fund, the total comes to more or less the same as the

---

[1] All figures taken from ISD, *Hong Kong: The Facts – Housing*, September 2013.

[2] www.housingauthority.gov.hk/mini-site/budgets13/14/en/view.html?f=5 note 5.2 on page 3, and Appendix F on page 10.

Hong Kong Housing Authority Budget, albeit the descriptions are not clear.

One thing however, is clear, there has been an enormous investment in public housing over the decades in Hong Kong. For example, the value of all land provided by the government for all public housing schemes, including HOS is HK$387bn (£29.7bn).[1] I emphasise: this is the figure for the land value only, and is in any case hidden away in an obscure note to the Accounts.

While the early PRH flats were pretty small (my siblings went on a tour of PRH housing in the early '80s and were embarrassed to discover one flat which was smaller than their bedrooms), and in most cases washing/cooking facilities were communal, the new flats are much more generous, and up to the standard one would expect in a developed economy. From the street, most recent flats differ only in the size of windows (which are smaller than in private flats), density and location, while flat sizes range from 18 sq m to 40 sq m (193 sq ft to 430 sq ft) depending on the number of bedrooms. All new flats have private kitchens, and up to two bathrooms within each unit. Developments now include shopping facilities, open spaces, gardens and schools on the estates. The overall appearance of these estates compares well with similar developments in the UK.

By any measure, this investment represents a major government intervention in the housing market, and places the HKSAR commitment to 'small government' in a different light.

In contrast, since the introduction of the Council House 'Right to Buy Scheme' in the 1980s by Margaret Thatcher,[2] provision of public housing in the UK has fallen to 18% of the total, of which 10% is owned and managed by local authorities, while 8% is owned and managed by social landlords such as Housing Associations.[3] No significant new council housing has been built since 1995, while some assistance is given to Housing Associations to develop some hybrid forms of social housing. In addition, in the UK, private developers are obliged to build

---

[1] Hong Kong Housing Authority Annual Report and Accounts 2012/13, note 19 b).

[2] British Prime Minister, 1979-91.

[3] Office for National Statistics, Table 101, Dwelling Stock: by tenure.

a proportion of 'affordable homes' which are made available to certain categories of 'essential workers' depending on the size of the development. Once built, these affordable homes are lost to the private sector.

Health

Life expectancy in Hong Kong is high (80.9 for males, 86.6 for females) while the infant mortality rate per 1,000 live births is 1.6.[1] In the UK the figures are 78.7 for males and 82.6 for females,[2] with infant mortality per 1,000 live births at 4.[3] Healthcare is provided in Hong Kong by both Public Hospitals (38), as well as Charitable, or Private Hospitals (11). The Public Hospitals are managed by the Health Authority, established in 1990, which employs 67,000 people. The total hospital beds per 1,000 population was 5, compared to 3 in the UK (in 2011), while the number of medical practitioners per 1,000 population was 1.8 in Hong Kong compared to 2.8 in the UK in 2012. Treatment in an outpatient clinic costs HK$45 (£3.50) which includes medicine as well as X-ray or other tests as required. Hospital stays are charged at HK$50 for registration and between $68 (non-acute) and $100 (acute) per day, with a scale of charges for any treatment required. In all cases, these fees are waived should the patient not have the ability to pay.[4] It is the policy of the HKSAR that: 'no one should be prevented, through lack of means, from obtaining adequate medical treatment'.[5] The Hospital Authority income is HK$47.1bn (£3.6bn), of which only HK$2.9bn (£223m) comes from fees.[6] The statistics on life expectancy speak for themselves. I don't propose to compare the levels of expenditure in the UK on the National Health Service (NHS), save to mention that the overall spending figure in the UK of £108.9bn in 2012/13 was

---

[1] ISD, *Hong Kong in Figures*, 2014.

[2] Office for National Statistics: Life expectancy at birth, on average in 2010/12.

[3] Office for National Statistics, 2012, published 28/2/14.

[4] All figures reported in: ISD, *Hong Kong: The Facts – Public Health*, December 2013.

[5] http://www.ha.org.hk, quoted on their Introduction page.

[6] HA Annual Report, 2013.

provided by 1.35m employees.[1] While visits to a doctor or hospital are free of charge in the UK, it is interesting to note the cost of prescription of drugs to most patients is £8.05 (HK$104.65) per prescription, or £104 per annum if you choose to pay for a twelve-month certificate.

Welfare

The level of public spending, as a percentage of GDP on welfare is so low, one would not imagine a very generous or highly developed network of social support for those fallen on hard times, or out of work.

In his book *Poverty in the Midst of Affluence*,[2] Leo Goodstadt is highly critical of the HKSAR's approach to welfare. While the colonial government was not overly generous, in the aftermath of the Asian Financial Crisis of 1997/8 the new administration managed to demonise the idea of welfare to an extent not seen elsewhere in the western world. For example:

> ... in countries where welfarism is practiced or a multitude of welfare services is provided ... many problems have emerged, such as unemployment, especially youth unemployment, domestic violence, shortage of elderly service ... Worse still it will undermine the people's resilience against adversities, which it is not conducive to the healthy development of the economy in the long run.[3]

These sentiments sprang from a Confucian tradition of self reliance, and an obligation on families to care for elderly relatives, which for a short period led to forcing applicants for help to obtain from family members a formal statement on non-provision of financial support – the so called 'bad son statement'.

There is a Social Welfare Department (SWD) in Hong Kong, whose budget in 2013/14 amounted to HK$54.7 (£4.2bn), having responsibility for cash assistance for individuals or households falling below a prescribed level. It provides Comprehensive Social Security Assistance (CSSA), as well as a Social Security Allowance

---

[1] http://www.nhs.uk/NHSEngland/thenhs/about/Pages/overview.aspx.

[2] Hong Kong University Press, 2013.

[3] Chow, Secretary for Health and Welfare, *Hong Kong Hansard* (HH), 29 March 2006, p.6103.

(SSA) for those over 70 years of age, or with a disability, which are not means tested.

Smaller schemes exist for criminal injury compensation or traffic accident victims, as well as child welfare services. The SWD also works with numerous non governmental organisations (NGOs) to provide assistance to young people with special needs, disabilities or those requiring rehabilitation in a number of circumstances[1].

For those wishing to study the workings of welfare provision in Hong Kong, and its limitations, Goodstadt's work is a good place to start, but I will not go into more detail here, save to observe that the origin of systematic 'welfare' in the UK can be traced to the Elizabethan Poor Law of 1601 – a reaction to the growing problems of poverty and famine arising from the first wave of land enclosures following the dissolution of the monasteries under Henry VIII. I should add that I noticed a number of people with disabilities begging on the street on my visit to Hong Kong in 2014. This is not something I had seen on previous visits, which suggests a decline in the level of care available through government or associated charities.

Andro Linklater has made a powerful study of the effects of land ownership,[2] and the imperative of new owners to have political power in order to defend their property. He points out that John Locke's defence of private property relies on the provision that it is acceptable only '... where there is enough, and as good, left in common for others'.[3] In the context of China, and by association Hong Kong, this principle has a long history. As Linklater says:

> it harked back to the fourth century BC when the Confucian scholar Mencius taught that farmers should be allowed exclusive use of their fields so long as they fed the nonfarmers in the community.[4]

---

[1] ISD, *Hong Kong: The Facts*, September 2013.

[2] *Owning the Earth*, Bloomsbury, 2013.

[3] John Locke, *Second Treatise of Government*, Chapter V, paragraph 33.

[4] *Owning the Earth*, page 373.

The conclusion of his argument is:

> The iron law of private property turns out to be a paradox. Although it promotes individuality, it only works by giving equal weight to the public interest.[1]

Ignoring the public interest in this context gives rise to the need for welfare, which comes in a variety of forms. In the UK, we can trace the abandonment of the public interest to the several periods of land enclosure in our history, by which access to common land, and rights to the commons in general, were expropriated by the larger landowners by Acts of Parliament. A detailed history of this process can be found in *The Village Labourer*.[2]

Private ownership and exclusive use without welfare gives rise to extreme poverty, as we can see in many developing countries around the world. In Hong Kong, private ownership and a resistance to welfare combined with less growth in the years after 1998 brought about a gradual rise in hardship, which the new Chief Executive recognises (see below).

Personally, I am not in favour of comprehensive welfare programmes, which seem to give rise to inefficiency and a dependency culture. I am confident that if more individuals have a fairer chance to use land to create wealth, they will be able to generate enough income by their activities to reduce the current reliance on welfare.

Addressing some of the shortcomings in the system of public revenue in Hong Kong might create a situation for individual enterprise to thrive enough to enable people to pay for services provided by a system of welfare in other jurisdictions. In other words, if you can fix the system, the need for welfare might disappear. By the same argument, if you can fix the system of high tax on individuals in the UK, and shift the raising of public revenue on to the value of land by a land value tax, you might be able to reduce the high welfare budget at the same time. A shift to raising public revenue by means of a charge against the locational value of all land would make land in general a less attractive

---

[1] *Owning the Earth*, final paragraph.

[2] J L Hammond and Barbara Hammond, *The Village Labourer, 1760-1832*.

'investment', and therefore reduce the price of land altogether. This would lower the barrier to entry which currently exists for many individuals around the world.

Problems associated with the high price of land

As I have begun to hint at, the HKSAR is not without its problems, some of which are directly impacted by the high cost of housing, which in turn is driven by the high cost of land.

Hong Kong's gini coefficient[1] at 0.537 in 2011, compares with the UK at 0.34 or Sweden at 0.25. It is not the worst in the world with some countries having coefficients over 0.65, but clearly Hong Kong is in the upper echelons of inequality.

Levels of poverty are also growing, with 1.3m people (19.6% of the population before benefit distribution, 15.2% after) living below the poverty line.[2] While these figures are difficult to compare with the UK given different methods of measurement, the picture is not so different, with 23% of the population in the UK 'at risk of poverty or social exclusion' in 2010.[3]

Given the large numbers of refugees arriving in Hong Kong after the Communist victory in China in 1949 (the population doubled by 1965, and again by 1995, while in the four years from 1948-1951, the population increased from 800,000 to two million), the second half of the twentieth century brought many signs of extreme poverty to the streets of Hong Kong. After concerted efforts to provide public housing, health and education, during that period, the 2013 report is an admission, perhaps for the first time, that more needs to be done to redress the balance of wealth distribution in Hong Kong. Indeed, the images of so called 'coffin homes', where rooms are divided by wire cages or wooden panels into 200 x 70cm bed spaces, are shocking.[4] With barely enough room to sit up, they illustrate the dire need for more public housing today. The Hong Kong Chief Executive recently admitted:

---

[1] A measure of wealth distribution, whereby at 0, all wealth would be equally shared by the population, whereas at 1, all the wealth would be held by one person.

[2] HKSAR Commission on Poverty, 2013.

[3] Eurostat EU SILC survey 2012.

[4] http://www.reuters.com/news/pictures/slideshow?articleId=USRTR38YE4#a=1.

> To alleviate poverty, the government must promote balanced eco-
> nomic development, poverty is not only an issue of the low-income
> population's hardship, but it also affects Hong Kong's harmony and
> stability, thus affecting its long-term competitiveness.[1]

As a result of all these factors, advocates of LVT have been
reluctant to cite Hong Kong as an example of the effectiveness
of the policy.[2] However, a careful examination of the practice in
Hong Kong is needed to understand how and why the deficiencies
have occurred.

There is no doubt that Hong Kong suffers from high land
values, and therefore high property prices, and it is often said that
the government pursues a high land price policy. A few Hong
Kong families have enjoyed the benefit of this policy – witness
the regular appearance of Hong Kong's property billionaires in
the worldwide annual surveys of wealth.[3] Hong Kong is not the
only country to celebrate high property prices, indeed rising
property prices are regularly lauded by politicians in the UK to
bolster confidence in economic recovery. This is done without a
thought for the next generation struggling to mount the so called
'property ladder', or those with no aspiration or possibility of
doing so. In both cases, the benefit of property ownership, which
can be used as collateral to raise finance and make investments
in wealth creating businesses is well understood[4]. What is less
publicised is the free ride afforded to owners of land, in terms of
the rising land values created by the presence and work of rising
numbers of people.

The fortunate early arrivals in Hong Kong who secured early
leases, or virtual freeholds – the 999-year leases – at fixed rents
have enjoyed for many years the unearned income from rents
afforded by the control of land. Their behaviour is no different
from landowners in the UK and around the world. They have
sought to embed their advantage, and continue to use their

---

[1] Hong Kong Chief Executive, Leung Chun-ying, 28/9/13, on publication of the Commission on Poverty report.

[2] See for example Alice Poon, *Hong Kong's Land Policy: a recipe for social trouble*, 2011.

[3] There are four from Hong Kong in the top forty Bloomberg Billionaires.

[4] Hernando de Soto, *The Mystery of Capital*, 2000.

property income to secure more land for development. Poon claims that Sun Hung Kai Properties owned a land bank comprising 41.9m sq ft of developable floor area, and 24m sq ft of agricultural land, while Henderson Land held 19.8m sq ft of developable floor area and 32.8m sq ft of agricultural land.[1]

While these 999-year leases (which also often enjoy fewer restrictions for development) are highly valuable, and generally consist of larger plots than more recent leases, their overall number is relatively low. Roger Nissim estimates that they make up only 1-2% of the total number of leases, a percentage confirmed by Kim Salkeld, a former head of the Land Registry in Hong Kong.

During my visit to Hong Kong, I was lucky enough to have a meeting with Patrick Kwok, Executive Director of Henderson Land. Our meeting took place on a very high floor of their offices overlooking the harbour – my ears popped several times in the two lifts we took to a plush meeting room with twenty or so chairs, and large teak table with all the latest conference gizmos, and a very thick carpet.

Mr Kwok was charming, and candid in his explanation of how the best developers work in Hong Kong. He confirmed the company policy of amassing agricultural land in the New Territories, and illustrated the benefit of doing so. At a site in Double Cove land was purchased in 1994 at HK$120 (£9) per sq ft. When construction began in 2009, the land had risen in value to HK$3,200 (£246) per sq ft, to accommodate a 21-block residential development with sea views designed by UK Architects Rogers Stirk Harbour. On completion the development commanded a value of HK$11,000 (£846) per sq ft on the saleable area.

In another illustration, this time for prime Hong Kong office development – the International Finance Centre (IFC) on Hong Kong island, Henderson paid a premium on Land Sale to the Hong Kong government of HK$5,300 per sq ft in 1996. The IFC is built on land reclaimed from the harbour, with one tower standing 88 storys high, and boasting 3m sq ft of office, shopping and hotel accommodation. After taking the risk of construction, with costs of HK$1,700 per sq ft, the value today is HK$25,000

---

[1] Alice Poon, *Land and the Ruling Class in Hong Kong.*

per sq ft. In contrast, in the year 2000, Sun Hung Kai paid only HK$1,700 per sq ft for the Kowloon International Commerce Centre (ICC) site due to a slow down in the economic outlook at the time. No doubt today, that value is similar to its shorter competitor on Hong Kong island.

Mr Kwok also gave a convincing reason for ever rising property prices in Hong Kong. Against a background of average demand for private residential units of 19,000 per annum,[1] since 2005 the market has only delivered a falling number of completions: from 17,300 to a low of 7,160 in 2009. This had climbed back to 13,550 in 2013, and an estimate of 15,820 in 2014.[2] In response, new land for housing has become a priority of the Hong Kong government. Chief Executive Leung Chun-ying announced that he would raise the target for housing unit completions by 40% over the next five years, with 60% of completions being Public Housing. The government promised to re-zone 152 sites, many close to the Chinese border, to encourage development of 215,000 new flats by 2019.[3] He also pledged to restart a programme of favourable loans available to residents of public housing units to encourage a move to private housing, which was abandoned in 2004.

There was a well documented fall in house prices soon after the handover of Hong Kong to China in 1997, with values falling by as much as 70% over the next five years.[4] No doubt many factors affected this fall, not least the Asian Financial Crisis which began in that year. However, the number of housing completions was well above the average demand referred to above from 1999 to 2004 inclusive – with 30,900 completed in 1999, and a peak of 31,000 in the year 2002. However, the first Hong Kong Chief Executive Tung Chee-hwa had made a new public housing programme the centrepiece of his post colonial administration,[5] and

---

[1] Centaline Property Agency research http://hk.centanet.com/icms/template.aspx?series=281&article=47117.

[2] HKSAR Transport and Housing Bureau forecast.

[3] Reuters, January 24 2014.

[4] Government Information Services (GIS), 17/10/2003.

[5] Alkman Granitsas, Land's End: Hong Kong Chief outlines Real Estate Policy in First Speech, FEER, 17 July 1997.

it could be said that the major property developers lost no time in defusing that potential threat to their dominant market position. Over the coming years, Tung was forced to backtrack from his initial ambition, which was a major factor in his eventual loss of authority, as Leo Goodstadt describes in his book *Uneasy Partners*:

> The political damage to Tung from the failure of his housing policies was critical because the entire community had been hurt: the property tycoons, the middle class owner occupiers, and those on the waiting lists for public housing.[1]

Could it be that some of Hong Kong's high house prices are due to good old fashioned supply and demand imbalances, rather than a conspiracy to maintain a high land price? Given the lack of awareness of the importance of land to economic considerations generally,[2] and to the specific impact in Hong Kong due to the unique land ownership arrangements, it is not surprising to find that the impact of certain policies were unforeseen. This often gave developers opportunity to profit, which might have been avoided with greater knowledge of the impact of land availability in Hong Kong.

For example, in 1984, the Joint Declaration between Hong Kong and China on the return of sovereignty to China, limited the amount of land that could be granted in any one year to 50 hectares,[3] although this could be varied by the new Land Commission if it felt the release of extra land was justified. This limit was imposed by the Chinese fear, that the Colonial government would seek to extract as much value as possible from Hong Kong, and take it with them before the date of reversion – these were often referred to as the 'golden eggs' at the time. To avoid this happening, proceeds from land sales in the period 1984-1997 were invested in the Land Fund, and as it turned out, the 50-hectare limit was in fact breached in every year up to the handover

---

[1] Leo F Goodstadt, *Uneasy Partners: The conflict between Public Interest and Private Profit in Hong Kong*, Hong Kong University Press, 2009.

[2] There are five entries for land in the index of the standard text book, Lipsey and Chrystal, *Positive Economics*, against 37 for capital, 8th edition, Oxford University Press.

[3] Paragraph 4, Annex III, Joint Declaration.

of sovereignty. By 1997, HK$197bn (£15bn) had been accumulated, which transferred to the Capital Works Reserve Fund after the handover.

That is not to say that the major developers did not hold almost monopolistic control over the supply of new housing units:

> In 1987 the nine largest developers accounted for 48% of that year's new supply of private residential accommodation. By 1991, this group's share of the new supply had risen to 84%.[1]

We will see over the coming years whether the new Chief Executive is more successful in supplying the obvious demand for affordable public housing, without causing a collapse in prices in the private sector.

How could a variation in land sale conditions help?

All this turmoil in the housing market in Hong Kong is familiar to residents of most western economies, where housing often forms the largest monthly expenditure in the family budget. In the latest house price indicators published by *The Economist*, Hong Kong has enjoyed (or should we say suffered) the highest percentage change in prices since Q1 2008 at 99.8%,[2] as well as having the most overvalued housing stock relative to rents at 79%. Should not the picture in Hong Kong (where all land is publicly owned, and an annual Government Rent is paid for the use of land) be rather different? The problem lies in the uneven and partial application of this annual charge for the use of land.

Putting aside the issue of Government Rent being applied to the rateable value of the building,[3] the problems in Hong Kong arise for a number of reasons. Perhaps the main issue relates to the supply of land, which is wholly determined by government policy. One could say in fact that there is no free market in land in Hong Kong, given that new parcels of land only become

---

[1] Quoted in Goodstadt above, taken from Hong Kong Consumer Council: *How competitive is the Private Residential Property Market?* 1996.

[2] *The Economist*/ Frothy Again/, August 30th 2014

[3] Henry George asserts that the annual charge should only apply to the value of the Land, not the building placed on it.

available when the government decides that new leases should be offered for tender. This is an artificial restriction. The government also controls the re-zoning of land for residential purposes, while the Urban Renewal Authority perhaps only responds to new development potential when approached by the existing lease-holder, rather than being more proactive.

David Webb, a former investment banker and now activist shareholder based in Hong Kong, argues that the problem lies more in the method by which use of land is purchased – a large premium being paid for a 50-year lease, with a small annual payment (3% Government Rent) thereafter. This means that at the time of purchase, 97% of the land value is paid in the initial premium, with only 3% being collected over the life of the lease. By extension, 97% of any increase in the value of land over the term of the lease accrues to the new property owner, while the government only collects 3% of that value per annum in Government Rent. Webb therefore suggests an alternative structure, a so called GR30 lease, where the Government Rent would be set at 30% per annum. To distinguish these leases from the current crop, he suggests referring to the 50-year lease at 3% as a GR3 lease, and older leases at fixed rents as GRF leases. The length of lease is immaterial, as I have shown above, because the practice has developed for the lease to be rolled over into a perpetual lease. Webb estimates this simple change would reduce land premiums by between 32 and 40%, depending on the type of housing unit to be built, and the location.[1]

For a detailed history of the development of leasing arrangements in Hong Kong, I can thoroughly recommend the first part of David Webb's paper published on his website,[2] some of which was invaluable in increasing my understanding of the mechanics of land ownership in Hong Kong, and much of which I have paraphrased. His suggestion for a modified form of lease exposes the issues involved most effectively, and his description of how the new leases would be valued (against the GR3 lease) is most revealing. He argues that such a change in leasing arrangements

---

[1] David Webb, *Hong Kong Land Lease Reform, Part 2*, 1st November 2010, http://webb-site.com/articles/leases2.asp.

[2] http://webb-site.com/articles/leases1.asp.

would generally reduce premiums, as the market would have to allow for a higher proportion of the land value being collected annually via the Government Rent at 30% of rateable value, to be paid over the lease term.

While this proposal would open up the market to smaller developers (given that leases would become more affordable), it does not provide the whole solution.

Alice Poon[1] also provides some insight into the ramifications of special arrangements arrived at in Hong Kong in relation to rural land in the New Territories, some of which go back to the original (1898) provisions of the lease from China. One of these was the provision that sons (not daughters) of the original, indigenous holders of land in the New Territory, should have the right to build a new house for themselves. This is now known as the Small House Policy, and is open to abuse. Who is to determine who may benefit from such rights, when there is no definitive list of the indigenous population going back to 1898? Once an individual has gained the right to a plot of land under this scheme, he is able to sell the right immediately to a developer at a good profit. David Webb has tackled this issue, and come up with a proposal as to how the government might wind down this otherwise open ended ability to profit from the rising price of land.[2]

Once again, careful negotiation in the lead up to the Joint Declaration led to an automatic right of extension for leaseholders until June 30 2047 (fifty years after the handover) for leases held on fixed terms without right of renewal up to 27th June 1997, with no additional premium to be paid. It could be said that this was a one way ticket to profit for the developers in possession of such leases.

Another random example of the means by which developers have profited from the rapid expansion of the urban area in Hong Kong relates to the development of the New Towns during the nineteen sixties, seventies and eighties. This is the 'letters A/B' system. The Hong Kong population at the time was expanding so rapidly, that a series of New Towns were planned at various places

---

[1] *Land and the Ruling Class in Hong Kong.*

[2] website.com/articles/smallhouse.asp 9/9/14.

in the New Territories such as Sha Tin, at the time a small fishing village on the road towards Fanling, a popular weekend retreat and golf course for Hong Kong's elite. The government needed to secure sufficient land from the farmers to build the towns.

I recall tortuous journeys on clogged single lane roads past paddy fields and the occasional leather tannery, the smell of which (not pleasant) is seared in my memory. It was another world from the bustling and over-crowded streets of Hong Kong, and we would be woken at dawn by cockerels from the neighbouring farms. We stayed in simple whitewashed bungalows with red tile roofs and cool tiled floors, with the smell of curry emanating from the kitchen for Sunday lunch! Most buildings in the villages were single storey, while the village of Fanling might have had some more substantial shops with accommodation above. In the surrounding hills one could see traditional family graves, with smoke often rising from freshly placed joss sticks.

Normally, if land is resumed by government for public purposes, cash compensation is paid. At the time, the government did not have sufficient cash to pay the landowners in the New Territories, so promises were made to offer other land to the owner at a later date. In the case of letter B agreements, for every five square feet of agricultural land resumed, two square feet of building land would be granted. While developers at the time might not have had a need for more building land, they could see the speculative advantage in accumulating these letters A/B agreements, whose price rose with the increasing population, and went about purchasing these agreements from the original holder. Once again, before the hand over, China insisted that all these agreements were rescinded. It was almost as if the Hong Kong government had to offer reverse premiums to the holders of letters A/B agreements to ensure that they were rescinded by the due date! Full details of this process can be found in both Poon[1] and Nissim.[2]

Today, many of these fields have disappeared under the New Towns, which consist of high rise, high density towers, with the

---

[1] *Ibid.*

[2] *Ibid.*

full array of shops, factories, offices and excellent transport links to the centre, accommodating hundreds of thousands of citizens.

We turn now to how a more equitable system of land holding might have developed, had the importance of land been recognised at the outset. According to the tenets of land value taxation, there should be no premium for the land. The only requirement from a public revenue point of view, would be an annual payment of a percentage of the bare land value, reassessed every year. This payment could continue to be called the Government Rent – it is in effect an annual charge for the value of services provided to any particular location by the public purse. The value of land, of course, will vary from location to location, and the percentage rate charged could have been determined by the needs of the government to satisfy their requirement for public spending.

In the case of Hong Kong, given the clear need to open up more land to the market, once truly public needs for land have been met, for example land for public infrastructure, recreation, public amenity space etc., the new land value rents could be set. The process would be perhaps to divide the remaining land into useable plots; the rateable values would be calculated on these plots; then an appropriate rate of Government Rent would be set for the use of these plots. Demand from potential occupiers would help determine the rateable values on new sites – with the age old question: 'What am I bid?' sometimes being the best determinant. Whether the rate of Government Rent is 3%, 30% or more, would be determined by a calculation based on how much revenue needs to be raised. It would be better to maintain flexibility in the rate set, assuming that other taxes and charges would be reduced or abolished, as the revenue stream from Government Rent increased: over time, and depending on the needs of government, the rate could reduce.

Thereafter any developer willing to pay the rent would be able to secure the lease, and follow the normal requirements of the planning system before commencing development of the land. Once the land has been developed, assuming the original lease is subdivided among the new owners of apartments, or buildings, the responsibility for paying the Government Rent would pass to the individual owners. Crucially, under the new arrangement, there would be no up-front premium for the lease, which would once again open up the market to new entrants – even to individuals wanting to secure their own lease, and build their own house. The only requirement would be the ability and willingness to pay the Government Rent, as well as complying with all relevant planning laws.

Restrictions on the use to which land is put could be maintained – for example, residential, industrial, agricultural – yes, there is still some agricultural land in Hong Kong! One significant feature of land use in Hong Kong is the amount of land occupied by Country Parks. This originated under the direction of Governor Murray Maclehose (another Scot!) in 1976, with the Country Parks Ordinance (Cap. 208) and the Marine Parks Ordinance (Cap. 76) in 1995. There are now 23 Country Parks, with good public access, which together with other Special Areas outside the parks, comprise 38% of Hong Kong's total land area. These parks attract over twelve million visits per year, significantly enhancing the quality of life for Hong Kong's residents.[1]

Naturally the permitted use would determine the rateable value for each plot of land as is common in other markets. No doubt a secondary market would evolve for individual plots, particularly once a building has been placed on the land. In effect, the new purchaser would agree a price for the building only, assuming that the full economic rent for the land is being collected through Government Rent. On completion of the transaction, they would also take responsibility for the payment of the rent. One side effect of such a scheme, would be to discourage the land banking activities of developers. Who would agree to pay the Government Rent for a plot, without developing some kind of economic activity or value in use on that site with which to pay the rent? The blight of empty plots in the middle of large cities (not so common in Hong Kong) might disappear – the 13-acre site of the old Battersea Power Station in London has been unused since its closure in 1983. Only now (in 2014) is it being developed by a Malaysian consortium for thousands of new homes, shops and offices, with generous help from the government in the form of a new tube line extension, designed to connect the site to the existing transport infrastructure.

---

[1] Nissim, page 99.

All previously leased land, and any buildings on it, whether they are offices, hotels or private apartments would continue to change hands at the market price. Given that the existing Government Rents on old leases are contractual, there would ensue another protracted period of transition in Hong Kong before all land was held under the same terms. The point at which the new terms for the use of land would come into effect, would be set by the expiry of the lease.

It may be that given the legacy of old fixed rent leases, an introduction of a new system of Land Sale without premium may not be possible without seriously distorting the market, but more research is necessary to examine the likely effect, and determine any necessary transitional arrangements.

Sadly, there has been very little public endorsement of David Webb's proposed reform of the leasing arrangements in Hong Kong, and even less real assessment of the unique benefits brought about by their system of landholding. It seems that Mr Webb has come up against the usual fear of change, and Richard Cullen laments 'the lack of institutionalised revenue/tax policy planning' in Hong Kong, pointing out that there is no 'high level, standing Tax Policy research infrastructure'.[1] He relates the repeated practice of forming ad hoc committees drawn from local business elites whenever any change is proposed. He says 'it is almost always the case with tax reform, that one can rely (on) a wide array of Status Quo Warriors to man the road blocks.' Another reason perhaps for the general lack of interest in how public revenue is collected in Hong Kong, is its staggering success: why tinker with a system which produces a healthy surplus year after year, and why ask questions, or waste money in research when you have so much in fiscal reserve!

While in the UK there is growing recognition of the potential value of a switch to LVT in newspapers[2], and by a growing number of politicians[3], the resistance to change remains strong.

---

[1] *Ibid.*

[2] For example, in many articles by Martin Wolf, Economics Editor of the *Financial Times*.

[3] For example, Andy Burnham, Labour, Caroline Lucas, Green Party, Vince Cable, Liberal Democrat, Nick Boles, Conservative.

Apart from this natural resistance to change, there would be no obstacles to the introduction of LVT in the UK. In fact, such a scheme of taxation has been on the statute books twice before, once in 1910[1] and again in 1931.[2] An essential precursor to any such introduction, would be an assessment of all land values and a change in the method of valuation for the various rating lists. There may also need to be a number of transitional arrangements to alleviate the introduction for people in particular circumstances, where a radical change to the tax system may introduce impossible liabilities. All of this could be investigated and resolved during any consultation period before the introduction of any new tax. All of these would be merely administrative changes, and would be grist to the mill for surveyors and civil servants. A common objection to such a tax is that it would be impossible to make a separate assessment of the 'land only' value. However, the fact is that separate valuations are given in Denmark for land and buildings in the rate assessments sent to house owners. Equally I have not witnessed a lack of interest in vacant pieces of land owing to the inability of surveyors to value sites consisting of 'land only'.

The key requirement to any such introduction would, of course, be a shift away from the existing destructive taxes. This would be essential, both to win public support, and to have any impact on the economic performance of the UK. If the introduction of LVT in the UK was simply seen as an additional tax, it would fail in its potential to transform the public finances. We can see in Hong Kong the beneficial effect of raising public revenue from land values in particular locations, even though the process is an unintended consequence of the system of land ownership in Hong Kong, rather than a planned and economically efficient method of taxing land values.

This analysis of Hong Kong's alternative sources of public revenue (arising from the leasing of land) has included some comparison of public services provided to the people of Hong Kong

---

[1] It was the main plank in the so called 'People's Budget' put forward by the Liberal Party. The tax was a casualty of the 1911 Parliament Act, which removed the power of the House of Lords to veto Bills from the Commons.

[2] Included in the Finance Act of 1931, but later neutered by the National Government.

compared to those services provided in the UK, as well as a detour to suggest some possible remedies to the problems caused by the method of leasing of land in Hong Kong. In the next chapter, we turn to one of the more remarkable examples of how a first class underground railway network was built for Hong Kong at no direct cost to the Hong Kong taxpayer, while at the same time increasing the revenue stream to the Hong Kong government after the initial phase of major investment.

This story is just another example of how public ownership of land, and the recognition of how public investment in infrastructure can enhance land values, may be used to benefit the whole community. A failure to recognise this mechanism, and devise a way to recoup the investment, leaves the rise in land value entirely in the pocket of the landowner.

5

Hong Kong's Mass Transit Railway (MTR)

HONG KONG is one of the most densely populated cities in the world with a total population in 2013 of 7.2m, crammed into an area of some 1100 square kilometres. This gives a total density of 6650 per sq km, but rising to 46,000 per sq km in the Kowloon area.[1]

It is therefore easy to conclude that some form of public rail transport system is going to make more sense than an extensive road infrastructure. While there are good roads and expressways, the vast majority of journeys are undertaken by bus, tram, public light buses, taxis and the Mass Transit Railway (MTR), as well as some overground suburban light railways serving the New Territories. The mostly underground MTR system was first mooted in the late sixties, and serious planning gathered pace in the early 1970s.

A compact network of 4 lines was proposed, and the first contract awarded by the Hong Kong Government to a Japanese consortium led by Mitsubishi under a $5bn contract. With this contract, although land would have been sold to the consortium to build the railway, no development rights were to be granted. However, as the oil crisis gathered pace, the consortium realised the cost overrun estimated at some 40% would cripple their effort, so they withdrew from the contract.

It was a critical time for the project, and the withdrawal of Mitsubishi might have led the government to conclude that the whole enterprise was foolhardy, which would have pleased both the sceptics, and those in Hong Kong averse to any public spending on such a vast scale.

---

[1] *Hong Kong in Figures 2014*, Census and Statistics Department, HKSAR.

I have tried to research who came up with the new scheme that in the event ensured that the project went ahead. For a brief outline, although one that does not acknowledge the source of the idea, I have to rely on the description by Lau Wah-sum, a civil servant who later joined the MTR finance department.[1] He refers to the then Governor of Hong Kong, Lord MacLehose, as well as to the then Chairman of HSBC, Michael Sandberg, working together on how to finance the new underground:

> Travelling the world, we saw that every city subsidized their systems. In the UK, we saw that when you build stations, the area around the stations could be developed. Then came the idea to connect the network: we must buy the land around the stations at greenfield prices and then develop property around stations. This would help finance the railway.[2]

The government responded by creating a government owned statutory corporation (MTRC), and lent it HK$800m as well as selling to the Corporation the land for the railway. Crucially, in a departure from the original contract with Mitsubishi, the MTRC was also given the development rights of land above the stations, and in particular was sold a large piece of land on which the Kowloon depot was to be built, for storage and servicing of the rolling stock. The Corporation was required to pay a 'pre railway' price for the land, but was then able to seek commercial partners in the Property sector, to develop the stations, and any offices, flats or commercial space above them. For the Kowloon Bay depot site, a land premium of HK$355m was paid to the government (in the form of new shares issued to the government by the MTRC rather than cash). A revised network of three lines was also proposed under the terms of the initial contract, with an estimated cost of $5.8bn.

In all cases, the lease of land granted to the MTRC was coterminous with the operating lease for the railway. In other words, should the licence to operate the railway be withdrawn at any time in the future, the lease to the land around stations

---

[1] Anneliesse O'Young, *Moving Experience: The MTR's first 36 years,* South China Morning Post Publishers Ltd, editor Deen Nawaz, 2011.

[2] *Op. cit.*, page 40.

would also be withdrawn, so that it could be sold to the new operator.

This was not a new method of financing railways. The London County Council used a similar scheme to build the Metropolitan Line, now part of the London Underground network in the 1930s, whereby land around the proposed stations was purchased by the company, and then sold to developers at a higher price, once the railway had been built. The difference in price paid for the land at the outset, and the price achieved on the subsequent sale, paid for the building of the railway. The pioneers of the railway network in the United States used the same process at the end of the nineteenth century to finance the expansion West, but since the growth of mass car ownership, no country has utilised this method as effectively as Hong Kong.

In the case of Hong Kong, the MTRC did not sell on all the land once the railway was built. In most cases, the stations were retained by the MTRC, as well as any commercial shopping centres above them, which were subsequently leased for rent to shops, banks and restaurants. Only the flats above the stations were sold. The MTRC continues to operate these shopping malls, and continues to collect the rent and service charges from the tenants. Many of the larger malls built above the stations, which now include cinema and other entertainment complexes become weekend or evening destinations for the residents and visitors to Hong Kong. Offices and flats above the podium level were sold to the developers, and in turn to individual buyers in the case of apartments. It seems an obvious model to follow, particularly where population density is so high. The people moving into properties above the stations would provide early patronage for the railways, as well as custom for the shops.

The first MTR line opened in 1979, with further openings in 1982 and finally the Island line in 1986. The lines were built by international consortia of engineering and construction firms, financed by export credits by the governments of the foreign firms involved, as well as several Corporate Bonds issued on behalf of the Company by large commercial banks. These loans were repaid by the sale of flats once construction had finished.

To give an idea of the scale of development above certain stations, I will take the first project, Telford Gardens, situated on the Kowloon Bay depot. It is a ten-hectare podium comprising housing for 25,000 people as well as an Olympic sized swimming pool, cinemas, parks, schools and shopping centres. The way it works is described in the introduction to MTR's history:

> The simplicity of the model is mind-boggling. The MTR is granted land development rights from the government. The MTR then buys the land which has not been developed at a greenfield land value and develops complexes around and above the stations and depots. The property increases in value after construction of the railway, and the profit reaped would be ploughed back into the railway.[1]

This process is now known as the Railway + Property model (R+P), and has continued to be used by the MTRC to build all subsequent lines in Hong Kong, including the airport extension.

In economic terms it is described as 'value capture', as clearly the land nearest to the railway station is going to command a higher price, given its convenience to those who live there, as well as the wealth that can be generated by operators of commercial premises including shops and restaurants close to the station due to the number of passengers passing their doors each day on their way to and from work.

It is also known as Transport Oriented Development (TOD), as the MTRC is clearly engaged in a planning function for the government of Hong Kong, whereby it plans new railway lines in tandem with development of New Towns, as well as the conversion of land use from now redundant industrial spaces to residential and office development, for example in the Tseung Kwan O development of recent years. Much of the information in this section has been gleaned from a study by Cervero and Murakami in 2008,[2] and is useful to help illustrate how it works.

In 2002, some 41% of Hong Kong's population lived within five hundred meters of an MTR station.[3] By 2013, there were over

---

[1] *Op. cit.*

[2] Robert Cervero and Jin Murakami, *Rail + Property Development: A model of sustainable transit finance and urbanism*, UC Berkeley Center for Future Urban Transport, May 2008.

[3] B S Tang, Y H Chiang, A N Baldwin and C W Yeung, *Study of the Integrated Rail-Property Development Model in Hong Kong*, The Hong Kong Polytechnic University, 2004.

twelve million daily passenger journeys by some form of public transport,[1] with 46% undertaken by MTR. In fact, over 90% of journeys taken by public transport on a daily basis utilised the MTR for some portion of the journey. This implies a high degree of integration, and stations are often designed to accommodate bus stops and taxi ranks. Although I am not familiar with the bus network, I am told it is efficient and cheap. Taxis are abundant in Hong Kong, and despite the language barrier, drivers generally know where they are going! My favourite form of transport in Hong Kong would have to be the tram – although being over six foot tall, I must bend when I venture upstairs. It is an ideal spot from which to observe daily life in Hong Kong as distinctive steel and wooden panelled trams trundle back and forth from Central to Happy Valley and beyond! Perhaps the most precarious form of transport is the public light bus, which can be hailed down on most roads, so long as there is a space inside. The sound of the engine straining up the Old Peak Road in first gear will be forever with me, much as the old Star Ferry bell indicating when the gate was about to close. All of these forms of transport are relatively cheap – except perhaps for the taxi – with the tram in particular costing a little over a dollar for most journeys.

The system has also been designed to give easy access to Hong Kong's many outlying open spaces, beaches and country parks, which were developed under the stewardship of Sir Murray (later Lord) Maclehose, as I mentioned in the last chapter.

For anyone living in a large city, proximity to public transport is vital, as commuting to work by car is reserved for only a privileged few. So proximity to the station commands a premium. The TOD model dictates that development at the central sites will be primarily office, hotel or commercial space, while at the outlying stations, the development will be primarily residential. The stations themselves will house some commercial space, taking advantage of the desire to pick up the shopping on the way home! The MTRC clearly exploits this factor, and the Cervero/Murakami study identifies premiums paid for apartments immediately above the stations in different locations ranging from 15% to 80% depending on various factors involved in each

---

[1] *Hong Kong in Figures.*

location – clearly open space, sea views etc can have a compensatory effect as you walk further from the station – as well as the method of calculation. The stations identified for this kind of intense development make great effort to separate passengers from other forms of transport, by introducing elevated walkways to take passengers directly from the station to either offices or apartments within walking distance, while at the same time, where appropriate incorporating local bus services, and car parks within the station perimeter. This means that passengers using a second form of transport to continue their journey, are encouraged to do so, while those only using the MTR do not have to do battle with other forms of transport on the streets to arrive at their destination. The people of Hong Kong are very proud of their MTR, and it is almost as clean (in 2014) as the day it opened, with no evidence of graffiti or litter associated with public transport systems in the West.

All the development taking place around and above stations has given the company enormous scope to diversify their income. On average, between 2001 and 2005 the MTRC generated revenue from the following sources:

Railway 28%
Property Development 52%
Property Investment and Management 10%
Non fare 10%[1]

By the late nineties, the MTRC had become so successful, not just at building railways but generating income that the Hong Kong Government decided to sell 23% of the company to investors through an Initial Public Offering (IPO). Some HK$30bn (£2.3bn) was raised for the government as a result of this sale.

Hong Kong prides itself on its adherence to Free Market principles, and a minimum of government involvement with business, and regards subsidy to business as anathema. The debate on the Mass Transit Railway Bill in the Bills Committee, which prepared the way for the sale of shares in the company,[2] included much

---

[1] Compiled from MTRC report and accounts, quoted in Cervero and Murakami.

[2] Legislative Council Library, record of meeting held on 18th November 1999.

argument over whether the granting of property development rights to MTRC constituted a government subsidy.[1] In response, the Director of Lands assured the committee that 'property development rights were granted to MTRC at full market value on a bare site basis' pre-railway. In this case, the government won the day, as it was deemed that no subsidy was being granted, and MTRC continues to pay the 'full market premium' for land used in its continued expansion of the network.

In 2012, MTRC generated profits of HK$13.6bn (just over £1bn), of which the majority went to the Hong Kong Government in the form of dividend. Of this profit, HK$3.7bn was derived from station commercial business, including shop rental and advertising, while a further HK$3.4bn was derived from other Hong Kong property rental and management businesses. Turnover amounts to HK$35.7bn (£2.7bn) and the company retained net assets of HK$144.5bn (£11.1bn).[2] Debt, mainly held by way of capital market instruments, stood at HK$23.3bn (£1.8bn) at the end of 2012.[3]

By contrast, Transport for London (TfL), which includes the underground network, London buses and light rail, receives an annual operating subsidy of over £1bn (HK$13bn), with operating income of £4.1bn (HK$53.3bn). Their net assets for the year 2011/12 were £16.1bn. TfL is currently engaged in a long overdue upgrade of the entire underground network, and the government grant for this work as well as the new Crossrail line in the year 2012/13 amounts to £5.5bn (HK$71.5bn). To be fair, TfL does have some other operating income, derived from commercial rents at stations as well as advertising on the network, and this amounted to £613m (HK$7.9bn) in 2012/13. In addition to their government subsidy, TfL have issued bonds in the capital markets, as well as holding other more conventional loans, and their total debt at 2012/13 was £7.5bn (HK$97.5bn), expected to rise to £8.5bn within two years.[4]

---

[1] For example, comments by Mr Ho Cun-yan, page 6, point 11.

[2] MTRC report and accounts 2012.

[3] *Ibid.*

[4] All figures taken from the *Annual Investor Update*, April 2013, published by the Mayor of London.

It seems that under the Railway + Property method, everyone is a winner. The people of Hong Kong benefit from a world class public transport system, where ticket prices are low by world standards – at zero cost to the public purse: quite the contrary, Cervero and Murakami estimate that for the period 1980 to 2005, the Hong Kong government received nearly HK$140bn (£10.7bn) in net financial returns:

> This is based on the difference between earned income ($171.8 billion from land premiums, market capitalization, shareholder cash dividends, and initial public offer proceeds) and the value of injected equity capital ($32.2 billion). Thus the government of Hong Kong has enjoyed tremendous finance returns and seeded the construction of a world-class railway network without having to advance any cash to MTRC. The $140 billion figure, of course, is only the direct financial benefit. The indirect benefits – e.g., higher ridership through increased densities, reduced sprawl, air pollution, and energy consumption, etc. – have increased net societal returns well beyond $140 billion.[1]

Clearly, this process of value capture, taking advantage of the natural phenomenon of rising land values in the vicinity of transport hubs, is much easier in a country where all the land is owned by the government. However, it would not be difficult to implement in countries where freehold land ownership is the norm. Many such jurisdictions also enshrine a process of compulsory purchase (in the UK) or eminent domain (in the US) of land where the national interest suggests it is necessary and useful. Indeed, this process was used to build the motorway network in the second half of the twentieth century in Britain, but has so far not included the retention of land by the operator for development, or a conferring of the development rights to the operator. The same process of compulsory purchase will no doubt be used to purchase land for HS2 (a new railway planned between London and Birmingham) but I suspect land will not be retained for development. Instead, in the UK, the benefit from public infrastructure investment has tended to accrue to the private owners of the land.

---

[1] Page 14, section 1.2.

In the case of the Jubilee Line extension on the London Underground, it is estimated that the £3.5bn investment, led to a £9bn increase in land values within the vicinity of the new stations.[1]

This process continues today, with the £16bn investment in Crossrail, a new high speed line running under the centre of London from Berkshire in the west to Essex in the east, which connects with several major London Underground stations along the route. Estate agents are benefiting from rocketing prices in the vicinity of the stations being developed to take the new trains, and newspaper articles already report on the money being 'made' by investors in property in the vicinity of the affected stations.[2]

The investment in Crossrail comes in the form of government grant drawn from general taxation. In addition a special Business Rate Supplement (BRS) is being collected from businesses (mostly tenants, not owners of property) along the route to help pay for the new line. Meanwhile, the land owners can only look forward with salivating lips for the higher rental income to be paid by the businesses flanking Oxford Street in London, where the main stations and interchanges with the underground system will emerge, once the line is open in 2018. GVA, the UK's largest independent property consultant produced a report in 2012 predicting a £5.5bn increase to property values along the route as a result of the investment. Mike Taylor, Director of GVA said:

> One of the biggest impacts of Crossrail will be on the commercial and residential property market with additional value of as much as £5.5bn generated along the route. Crossrail will have a distinct impact on the residential property market not just in London but also several areas in Essex and Berkshire. As a result of significantly improved transport connections, areas such as Abbey Wood, Woolwich, Ealing Broadway and Southall are highlighted as future places to watch. Crossrail is more than a new rail link, it will be the catalyst for regeneration and a key driver in maintaining London's position as a leading global city.[3]

---

[1] Stephen R Mitchell and Anthony J M Vickers, *The Impact of the Jubilee Line Extension of the London Underground Rail Network on Land Values*, Lincoln Institute of Land Policy, 2003.

[2] *The Sunday Times*, Home section, 24/8/14.

[3] *GVA report : Crossrail Property Impact Study*, October 2012.

The study predicts a 6% increase to rental rates on commercial property, a 10% increase in capital values over the next decade on office space, as well as a 25% rise in central London residential property values in areas close to the stations. Apart from the tenants who are paying the Business Rate Supplement (BRS), how much are the beneficiaries of this bonanza contributing to the cost of the development? The only mechanism available to the UK government is Capital Gains Tax, which is only collected on the sale of an asset, and does not apply to the primary residence of any individual home owner. Given the evidence available from the Jubilee Line extension, one suspects that these estimates (of increases in value and income) will prove to be on the low side.

There are only four major commercial contributors to the cost of Crossrail: Heathrow Airport Holdings (operators of Heathrow Airport, which will be served by a spur line from the main Crossrail line) who will contribute £70m. The Corporation of London, which owns an extensive portfolio of properties in the City, and elsewhere in central London; with no shareholders, the Corporation has lobbied government over the last twenty years to build Crossrail, and promised to make an advance investment of £200m, knowing the reward would follow. They will also seek £150m of contributions from other businesses, and has guaranteed £50m of these. Canary Wharf Group has agreed £150m towards the cost of the new Canary Wharf station, and Berkeley Homes has agreed to construct a 'station box' for a new station at Woolwich, which will no doubt serve the new residents of their own developments in the Woolwich area.[1]

TfL has also sold 'surplus land' to raise a total of £444m to help pay for Crossrail![2]

Hong Kong's MTRC continue to use the R+P method to plan and build new lines, and further enhance the network for the people of Hong Kong. There are currently five new lines or extensions under construction, with a further three projects in consultation periods. The company is now an international business, with much of their focus directed towards operations in China, as Hong Kong gradually integrates with Guangzhou and

---

[1] http://www.crossrail.co.uk/about-us/funding#.

[2] TfL, Annual Investor Update.

the wider Pearl River Delta. MTRC also operates some overground lines in London on behalf of TfL as well as in Stockholm. In July 2014, MTRC won the contract to operate Crossrail in London, against fierce competition. The contract is worth £1.4bn over eight years, with an option to extend for a further ten years.[1] So to the extent that MTRC profits from operating Crossrail, the passengers on this railway in London will be paying for a proportion of public goods and services for people in Hong Kong, through the dividend payments MTRC makes to the HKSAR.

At a meeting in March 2014 with Sharon Liu, Chief Town Planning Manager of MTRC, she confirmed to me that when a new project is proposed, the first question is:

> How much land do we need to cover the cost of building the railway?

Such a simple sentence, but it encapsulates the logic behind the whole process!

This calculation is then the subject of negotiation with the Hong Kong government, in terms of how much land will be released under a new land grant, to enable the MTRC to start negotiation with developers, to determine what level of tender will be forthcoming for the right to build and sell or lease the apartments and office blocks within the curtilage of the land grant. To illustrate the balance of power, in the case of Lake Silver at Shatin, the agreed profit share was split 93% to MTRC, and 7% to the developer, in this case Sino Land. In other examples, the split was a more normal 55%/45% for The Palazzo also at Shatin, or 31%/69% for Festival City.[2]

Before moving on to discuss the relevance of Singapore to this subject, and to demonstrate that the development of the MTR was not a one-off situation, I would like to share the development of Hong Kong's new airport with you.

Hong Kong's previous airport Kai Tak, was built on reclaimed land adjacent to Kowloon (one of the areas with the highest population density in Hong Kong), with the runway projecting

---

[1] TfL Press Release, 18th July 2014.

[2] MTRC report and accounts.

into the sea. The approach, depending on the wind direction either afforded passengers a close up view of washing hanging out to dry on the rooftops of apartments close to the airport, after clearing the jagged hill tops of the range separating Kowloon from the New Territories and following a rapid descent, or the sensation of landing on water, until the wheels made contact with the tarmac, and the runway came into view beside the 'plane! For new arrivals, it was hair raising to say the least!

In typical Hong Kong fashion, a new airport was planned to allow for a projected expansion of both passengers and freight consequent on the rapid development in China. This was to be built on reclaimed land on the larger, but sparsely inhabited island of Lantau, with road and rail connections to both Kowloon and Hong Kong island by newly built bridges. The Airport Authority was established in 1995, to be responsible for the operation and expansion of the new airport as a wholly owned statutory body of the HKSAR. Building the airport involved a HK$50bn (£3.8bn) investment in one of the largest engineering projects in the world at the time, to create a two terminal, two runway operation. A third runway, and further HK$12bn investment, is planned over the coming years. The airport commenced operations in 1998, and is within five hours' flying time of half the world's population. In 2013, 59.9m passengers used the airport (HKIA) and 4.12m tonnes of air cargo passed through Hong Kong. HKIA is connected to about 180 destinations, including 44 in the Mainland, through over 1,000 daily flights by more than 100 airlines.[1]

In the year to March 2013, the airport delivered profit of HK$5.6bn on turnover of HK$13.1bn, with a final dividend going to HKSAR of HK$4.4bn or £338m. Once again, almost half the revenue is derived from service operating licences, commercial rents (for the airport shops) and advertising. On top of the dividend paid to the government, the HKIA paid HK$1.1bn in tax, primarily Profits Tax.

And once again, the land on which the airport stands (most of which was reclaimed from the sea), was sold to the Authority on a 'Land Grant' lease for the 62 years from 1995 to 2047 (the point at which the fifty-year period for the Basic Law arrangements

---

[1] http://www.hongkongairport.com/eng/business/about-the-airport/welcome.html.

expire). In this case, a nominal premium of HK$2000 was paid, while the land formation cost was borne by the Authority, and is being amortised over the term of the lease; the net land formation cost stood at HK$11.3bn (£869m) at end of March 2013 in the HKIA balance sheet.[1]

In summary, the people of Hong Kong have gained an award winning[2] airport at no cost to the government, and at the same time created an income stream for the government which reduces the need to raise public revenue from more conventional sources such as Salaries Tax or VAT (GST).

---

[1] HKIA Annual Report, March 2013.

[2] Skytrax, World's Best Airport awarded to HKIA eight times since 2001.

6

Singapore

IN RESEARCHING for this essay, I discovered Hong Kong's Sovereign Wealth Fund, controlled by the Hong Kong Monetary Authority (HKMA), which I mentioned earlier. At the same time, I discovered a list of other Sovereign Wealth Funds, and was struck by a number of the entries. Most Wealth Funds are derived from the revenue of oil and gas or other natural resources. Norway tops the list with assets of US$893bn derived from oil.[1] There were six large funds whose assets were not derived from natural resources, within the top ten funds by value:

> China Investment Corporation US$652.7bn;
> SAFE Investment Company (China) US$ 567.9bn;
> HKMA (Hong Kong) US$ 326.7bn;
> Government of Singapore Investment Corporation US$320bn;
> National Social Security Fund (China) US$ 201.6bn;
> Temasek Holdings (Singapore) US$177bn.

It seemed incredible that two tiny island nation states in Asia (Singapore and Hong Kong) could amass such assets in the space of forty odd years, with no natural resources to speak of apart from location, and a combined population in 2012 of 12.4m.[2]

I began to wonder if this was just a coincidence, or whether each country had certain features in common. I will refer to China in more detail in the postscript, but the most obvious common feature in both Hong Kong and Singapore, was the system of land holding. I would also acknowledge that both countries in the modern era have enjoyed (or suffered) rule by a single

---

[1] http://www.swfinstitute.org/fund-rankings/ August 25, 2014

[2] World Bank 2012

authority in that time. In Hong Kong a British Colonial Governor followed by an appointed Chief Executive; in Singapore again a British Colonial Governor followed by an elected Prime Minister, whose party, the People's Action Party has won every election since 1959. The Singapore government is recognised as being competent and free from corruption, but freedom of speech is limited and opposition discouraged. China of course, is a one party state.

All three have enjoyed enormous economic growth, and GDP per capita in Singapore now exceeds that of the United States, with Hong Kong not far behind.[1]

Singapore now comprises 716 square kilometres (135 sq km have been added through land reclamation), about a third smaller than Hong Kong, and is an island at the tip of the Malaysian peninsula, with some smaller outlying islands to the south and east. Largely flat, it overlooks one of the busiest shipping routes in the world, with traffic from China, Indonesia and Japan on its way to Europe, India and Africa. Although Singapore has been continuously inhabited for two millenia, it was a British Colony from 1826 to 1963, and became independent from Malaysia in 1965. The majority of the population (75%) is ethnically Chinese, highly educated, and the country is a major trading and financial centre in the region.

The 2013 Index of Economic Freedom ranks Singapore (behind Hong Kong) as the second freest economy in the world.[2] Singapore shares many of Hong Kong's other attributes – low personal tax, high GDP per capita, a high gini coefficient 48.1,[3] low unemployment, and consistent growth over the last forty years.

What most descriptions of Singapore fail to highlight is the high degree to which the government of Singapore retains ownership of the land. The Singapore Land Authority (SLA) is the custodian of 140 sq km, around a fifth of all the land, on which over 5,000 buildings are placed. It continues actively to purchase

---

[1] Penn World Table, University of Groningen. Real GDP per person at PPP.

[2] Heritage Foundation/*Wall Street Journal*.

[3] World Bank, 2008.

land for development, particularly to enhance the public infrastructure.[1] When it comes to reselling that land, however, it does so on the same model (leasehold) as operates in Hong Kong.

Altogether, 58% of land in Singapore is State Land, when leaseholds sold to private operators is taken into account. Land for sale is offered every six months, on a reserve list system on the basis of which developers are able to offer a price for particular leases. If the offer is above the reserve price set by the department, the piece of land is then opened for sale by tender to other developers. Some sites are offered immediately for tender under the confirmed list. Once again, the 'land sale' is actually for a lease on a particular piece of land. Typically residential sites are offered on 99-year leases, while commercial sites are offered on 60-year leases. In each case, the full details of the permitted development are advertised in the lease, including site area, plot ratio and the gross development area permitted.

My analysis of the Singapore Government income and expenditure account reveals a very similar set up to the General Revenue Account in Hong Kong. You will be relieved to hear that I do not intend to go into the same level of detail, save to say that like Hong Kong, the Singapore Operating Revenue generally runs a surplus − S\$5.29bn in 2013 (£2.6bn) before transfers to Funds and net investment returns.[2] Total expenditure in that year was S\$51.7bn (£25.8bn) or just over 15% of GDP.[3]

As in Hong Kong, Corporation Tax is the single biggest contributor to the operating revenue at 22% of the total, while Assets Tax (on Property and Estates − although no Estates duty has been collected since 2008) comprised 7% of revenue. Many political parties around the world advocate taxing wealth, but few do so directly, preferring instead to increase taxes on income. Thomas Piketty[4] also advocates taxing wealth as a means to tackle

---

[1] Figures taken from the SLA annual report, 2013

[2] Singapore Government Analysis of revenue and expenditure, published on budget day, February 2015. Singapore dollars are converted at S\$1 to GBP£0.50.

[3] *Ibid.*

[4] Author of *Capital in the Twenty-First Century*, 2013.

inequality, but again, suggests this is done by increasing the marginal rates of tax on income.

Personal income tax raised 13% of the total. A further 7% was raised through Stamp Duty, which includes a levy on property transactions.[1]

Singapore Income/Expenditure	Actual 2013 S$bn	% of total
Operating Revenue	57.02	
Corporate Income Tax	12.68	22
Personal Income Tax	7.69	13
Withholding Tax	1.15	2
Statutory Boards Contributions	0.53	1
Assets Taxes	4.18	7
Customs and Excise Tax	2.19	4
Goods and Services Tax (GST)	9.51	17
Motor Vehicle Tax	1.65	3
Vehicle Quota Premiums	2.72	5
Betting Taxes	2.38	4
Stamp Duty	3.93	7
Other Taxes	5.25	9
Other fees and charges	2.9	5
Others	0.25	0
		100
Total Expenditure	51.73	
Operating Expenditure	39.72	
Development Expenditure	12.01	
Primary Surplus	5.29	

Property taxes in Singapore are assessed on the estimated annual rent of the property at a percentage of the annual value.

For owner-occupied properties, since January 2014, there is a progressive tax rate starting at 4%, rising to 15% for annual values in excess of S$130,000. For commercial, and industrial properties the rate is 10% of annual value for land. For non-owner-occupied residential properties, once again, the tax rate is progressive,

---

[1] *Ibid.*, although these figures are based on revised estimates for 2013.

starting at 10%, and rising to 19% for annual value in excess of S$90,000. The amount raised per annum varies with the annual valuations, so the actual revenue from Assets Taxes in 2008 was S$1.9bn, rising to S$4.2bn (£2.1bn) in 2013. Note the higher rates for buy to let properties, against owner-occupied properties.

Other sources of government income fall outside the operating revenue schedule, in other words, are not included in the table above, and include various fees and charges (S$5.2bn), investment and interest income (S$7.1bn) and capital receipts (S$18.4bn)

Included in the capital receipts, the revenue from land sales in 2012 was S$18.3bn (£9.1bn) – this equates to 36% of the total operating revenue in that year, but is not classified as taxation, although it is undoubtedly public revenue. Receipts from land sales go into reserves, which can in turn be spent on land reclamation, creating underground space or land and building acquisition for further development.

I have been unable to find the detailed revenue from Land Sales going back to previous years, although I do have the figure for 2009 (where the amount was a paltry S$4bn). Under standards set by the International Monetary Fund (IMF), public revenue from interest, investments and capital receipts should be included in public statements of government income and expenditure, and the IMF have prepared figures including these receipts going back several years. To be fair, the Singapore government also publishes these statistics, albeit not on Budget Day. The all-inclusive IMF standard statistics show that in the eight years from 2005 to 2012, a surplus of S$187bn was generated from these sources in Singapore. In each year, the amount raised varied from only S$2.9bn in 2009 to S$36.2 in 2012 – the year when over half of this additional revenue came from Land Sales.[1] One can only assume that these surpluses are invested in the two sovereign wealth funds owned by the Singapore Government.

These sorts of surplus, year after year, would be the envy of most governments in Europe, the Americas and Africa without revenue streams from natural resources such as oil. And don't forget, these surpluses do not come from general taxation, but can be considered as additional public revenue from non-conventional

---

[1] Singapore budget documents, *DOS Statistical year book*, 2012.

sources. It gives the government of Singapore great flexibility to promote major infrastructure projects, perhaps at times when a boost to GDP is required due to market failure (recession, or international financial crisis). We can also see that the Singapore government can rely on investment income and interest, or transfers between funds to plug any shortfall in regular tax revenue during economic downturns. Also it does not have to rely on bankers or the markets to raise money to fill any gap between income and expenditure. In the UK, we rely on the Public Sector Borrowing Requirement (PSBR), which is now a regular feature on Budget day. Neither, of course, is Singapore required to meet interest payments on government debts from 'normal' tax revenues.

In the recent articles and obituaries marking the death of Singapore's founding Prime Minister Lee Kuan Yew[1] no mention is made of these special arrangements for land, nor the Government's heavy involvement in Singapore's strategic industries. Only his encouragement of foreign investment, and free trade are worthy of comment in the economic sphere.

Surprisingly, the Singapore government spends the biggest percentage of its budget on Defence at 12% of the total, with Education just behind at 11% of the total. Transport and Health are also important with each category getting 6% of the total. I cannot comment on the perceived threat to Singapore which elicits such a high degree of spending on Defence, but Singapore joins Hong Kong and China (Shanghai) in the top three places of educational achievement in Mathematics, Science and Reading.[2] Perhaps the experience of invasion by Japan during the Second World War is still etched on their collective memory, and as an independent sovereign nation maybe they feel threatened by the proximity of both Malaysia and Indonesia.

If Hong Kong were an independent nation, it too would no doubt have to spend a similar proportion of the government revenue on defence. This saving contributes to the low level of public spending as a proportion of GDP in Hong Kong. The areas of Hong Kong occupied by the colonial military bases are now

---

[1] 23rd March 2015.

[2] PISA results published by the OECD, October 2014.

reserved for the People's Liberation Army (PLA), but clauses in the Basic Law in force until 2047, confines the soldiers to barracks! Significantly, this military land has not been released for development, and will in future either house a larger outpost for the PLA, or provide a significant windfall to the public purse, if it is made available for development.

Another feature of Singapore worthy of note, is the high percentage of people living in so called HDB (Housing & Development Board) flats. Setting up the HDB was one of the first steps taken by the Singapore government after independence to solve a perceived housing crisis, with many residents living in slum conditions. Today, over 80% of Singapore residents live in HDB accommodation[1]. While the HDB assembles the land, plans and contracts the building of the housing estates, residents are able to purchase these flats, rather than renting which is more typical of other public housing schemes. Some 90% of HDB residents own (at least partially) their flats.

Naturally, HDB flats are cheaper than private housing developments, and subsidies are available for those on lower incomes to assist first time buyers. For example, a three-room property at Matilda Court in Sumang Lane, due for completion in 2018, is on offer for S$186,100, with 65 sq m of living space, for a 99-year lease. Up to 25% of the price can be eliminated by subsidies for eligible applicants. Residents can also use money accumulating in their Central Provident Fund[2] (CPF) accounts to make the downpayment, and pay mortgage installments on HDB purchases. Particular rules apply to all these arrangements, I won't go into detail, but there is, for example, a secondary market for HDB flats, and extensive programmes to improve some of the earlier developments. Some of the newer developments have been constructed in partnership with private developers, and one (The Pinnacle@Duxton) features a Skybridge on the 50th floor, with spectacular views over the city, featuring gardens which are open to the public as well as residents.

There is a lively debate in Singapore about what will happen at the end of the 99-year lease period, which is still some forty to

---

[1] www.hdb.gov.sg.

[2] A mandatory retirement savings scheme for employees in Singapore.

fifty years off for some of the older developments. Will the government simply take back the property from the lease holder without compensation? Some of this apprehension is being allayed by a programme of the so-called Selective en-bloc Redevelopment Scheme (SERS) whereby existing leaseholders in older blocks in need of modernisation or replacement with higher density accommodation, are offered incentives (and a new 99-year lease in a new block) to give up their existing lease. I am confident that before too long, the Singapore government will act to resolve this issue. One option, short of a rolling SERS programme, would be to roll over existing leases in return for payment of an annual rent – similar to the Government Rent at 3% per annum that now applies in Hong Kong on so-called perpetual leases. The percentage charged could be proportionate to the needs of the Singapore government income required to cover public expenditure needs, and could gradually replace other taxes on consumption or income.

On the other hand, perhaps we are so used to the idea in the west of freehold ownership, and the right to pass on property to the next generation, that we cannot think clearly about this issue of perpetual ownership. Why do we assume that property should pass automatically to the next generation? Is this fair, or justifiable? After all, few individuals are likely to need somewhere to live on this earth for more than 99 years once they leave the parental home. The method by which property passes from generation to generation can in some cases perpetuate social elites, and lead to entrenched inequality and lack of social mobility. Would it be better for each generation to 'start from scratch' in finding somewhere to live? In the case of Singapore, there will be in the future, a constant source of new flats to choose from, with the expiry of existing leases after 99 years.

Looking at the reality of inheritance in the UK, for any Estate over £325,000 there is tax to pay at 40% – which is becoming increasingly common in London and the South East of England, due to the rising values of property. Surely this is just a convoluted means by which the government claws back some of the publicly created value in location, upon the death of an individual? Quite a hefty price to pay in one lump sum, when it could be collected over time, in smaller amounts. The knock on effect of this arrangement is that the next generation is forced to borrow large sums to take out a mortgage on property, which often is not repaid until the balance of the inheritance from one's parents is received after tax. Is it not more honest to offer each generation a new 99-year lease at a subsidised price, on the condition that the property is handed back for the next generation when the individual has no further need of it? If this is pushing the sense of individual freedom and entitlement to property ownership too far, a simple annual charge (LVT) on the publicly created value on any particular location could easily replace inheritance tax (and a good many others besides!)

A friend of mine, who lived in Singapore for twenty years adds his experience and comments as follows:

> Obviously I don't know about how the HK 'public' housing market is but do know a bit more about Housing Development Board, of which I am sure you can find a lot about online. I think HDB started in the late 1970s as a way to get people out of sub-standard low density 'kampong' housing into higher density, solidly built housing. As well as accommodating a growing population it would free up land for commercial/industrial development – necessary for the Singapore growth plan (and it was all planned).
>
> HDB housing is government controlled/developed/subsidised but differs from public housing in most parts of the world in that you have to buy it and own a 99 year leasehold property. It is not given to anybody. The rules are tweaked all the time (even since we bought in 2001) but basically every Singapore citizen has the opportunity to buy two newly built (subsidised building cost) HDB properties (one cannot own two concurrently) during their lifetime. You have to be over a certain age and/or married to qualify to buy one of these new (below market value because of the subsidy) properties and must own it for 5 years before you can sell it. Once you have sold, you then may be eligible to buy your next new one and the same conditions apply. Not everybody ends up taking advantage of this right to get the two new builds, because there are some limitations on location as the central areas have already been pretty much fully developed, and even in the HDB market, location is important/valuable. Singaporeans and Permanent Residents – the latter don't get the new flats, it's a way to incentivise people to take citizenship – can buy and sell (but own no more than one at a time) HDB flats in the open resale market (ie older flats).

That is where (as Permanent Residents) we bought ours (in the secondary market) for S$418k and sold in early 2012 for about S$730k; I think the private housing market had advanced even further over the same period. Ours was considered a very central location. I sense today that new build (subsidised) HDB prices range from $250-550k and resale values are between $350k to $950k today depending on size/location of flats.

Sizes range from about 60m² to 115 m² and have between 1-3 bedrooms although some people then renovate the interiors to create an additional bedroom from the standard provision. 2-3 bedrooms are the most prevalent of course.

When we bought we were allowed to use as much as 80% of our provident fund towards the purchase price of the flat (i.e. deposit and equity) and the only lender for HDB at that time was the Central Provident Fund (CPF) from whom one could borrow the balance at what must have been the lowest interest rates available (lower than any bank mortgage). Very clever really as people borrowed their own money and paid higher interest than the provident fund was returning, so it made for a self managing, risk free provident fund pool. Since then, as the government has worried about too much of people's provident fund being linked to housing equity, the amount of the provident fund that could be used for housing has been reduced and banks are now allowed to lend for the balance of HDB investment. The great thing when the CPF was the lender is that you could simply increase/decrease your mortgage payments each month depending on the cash flow provided by your salary and this extended/decreased the term of your mortgage. There were no admin fees for changes or questions asked. I think we had about $200k in our provident fund when we bought that we used for equity and we paid off the balance $200+k in about 7 years, only using our ongoing provident fund contributions (100% of which which are tax free) to make the repayments. When we sold we had to pay our provident funds back into CPF where funds of about S$550k sit today awaiting our retirement (we can get them back if we give up our permanent residency or reach the age of 65 when a certain amount is used as a retirement annuity and a certain amount gets released to us in a lump sum.

The key thing to the success of HDB (and people taking pride in their estates) is that it was no free handout. You buy, the value grows, you benefit. Furthermore, of course, the instant capital gain the government hands Singaporeans for their two new flats (realised when they sell the 'new' allocation into the open market after a minimum of 5 years), makes Singapore citizenship valuable and is sometimes said to explain why so many Singaporeans living in HDB flats still drive around in Mercedes E class vehicles. The cars seem to cost around the same as the capital gain people make when they sell their first HDB flat and as you know Asians value the status symbol provided by a Mercedes!

It seems that this arrangement is a win/win for both government and residents. No doubt the land value of the old low rise Kampongs which made way for the new HDB blocks increased enormously as a result of the higher density of land use. In his description, my friend also neatly encapsulated the saving/pension arrangements (CPF) for all Singaporeans able to work.

Either way, the HDB programme is an astonishing piece of central government planning and social engineering for a country that enjoys second place in the Heritage Organisation's index of economic freedom[1]

Just a quick note to fill out what the CPF is, and how it works. It is a compulsory and comprehensive method for Singaporeans to save for retirement, as well as education and healthcare. It was established in 1955 on principles of self reliance, and a determination for Singapore not to become a welfare state. Both employees and employers make contributions to the individual CPF accounts. The CPF pays fixed rates of interest on the money invested in the individual accounts. In 2013, the interest rates were 2.5% for the Ordinary account, and 4% for the Special and Medisave accounts, with an additional 1% on the first S$20,000 and S$60,000 respectively. Over the years, the CPF has become more sophisticated, and from 1997, some of the money can be used by citizens to make their own investment choices in some circumstances. The contributions to the fund are set at higher rates in early life – 17% for employees and 20% for employers, meaning a total of 37% of salaries are invested in the person's CPF account each year. For over '50s the rates of contribution drop to 35% overall, and 16% for the over '60s.[2] The total assets of the CPF in 2013 were S$255bn, of which members accounts held S$252bn.[3] The Board of the CPF is responsible for the investment

---

[1] www.heritage.org/index/ranking.

[2] Central Provident Fund contribution rates for 2015.

[3] CPF annual report and accounts for the year ended December 2013.

decisions for the majority of the funds held under management. The majority of the fund is invested in Singapore Government Securities (S$250bn) with the balance in a variety of Statutory Board bonds, Corporate bonds and equities.[1] So the government of Singapore forces its citizens to invest for their retirement. It then borrows this money at fixed rates of interest by issuing Government Bonds to the Fund.

Just a brief note too, on the two Sovereign Wealth Funds referred to at the start of this chapter.

The smaller of the two, Temasek Holdings, was established in 1974, to take over the assets previously held directly by the Government of Singapore, which included Singapore Airlines, a shipyard originally set up by the British government for the Royal Navy, Singapore Telephone Board and a number of smaller government agencies supplying goods and services to the government. The idea was to operate these companies and assets on more commercial lines at arms length, although the holding company (Temasek) is wholly owned by the Government of Singapore. The initial value of investments taken on by Temasek was S$354m, mainly holdings in Singapore companies. The current value of assets is S$223bn, with investments and offices in all the major financial centres around the world. Quite a good track record, by any standard!

The Government Investment Corporation (GIC) was set up in 1981 to manage Singapore's foreign reserves. Although it does not publish annual accounts of assets, income or expenditure for fear of revealing the levels of Government reserves to the markets, it does now (since 2008) publish its annual rate of return going back twenty years. The Sovereign Wealth Fund Institute, therefore can only estimate its value (US$320bn) with the help of Morgan Stanley, by looking at its activities over the years, estimating capital growth and revenues generated from investments. Once again, it is wholly owned by the Government of Singapore.

We can conclude this quick summary of Singapore's tax and public revenue regime by highlighting not only its effectiveness in generating government reserves, but also in fostering enterprise

---

[1] *Ibid.* Note 7, Investments.

and economic growth for the people of Singapore. Another example of a country with no debt (other than to its people), high growth, and low tax, with a method of generating further public revenue from it's rising land values.

7
Conclusion

THE INITIAL aim of this book was to provide students of the Economics with Justice courses with an example of a place where the economic rent of land was collected through a land value tax. Our journey has not exactly provided that example, given the random and accidental way in which the regime for taxation and public revenue collection has developed in Hong Kong. However, there are some interesting elements of the system both in Hong Kong and Singapore, which have produced a very pleasing outcome.

If the purpose of economic policy is to create a country with balanced budgets, ample reserves, high quality education, good transport infrastructure, low unemployment, sustained and higher than average growth, then both Hong Kong and Singapore seem to perform quite well. At the heart of both cities' approach to this task is an understanding of the value of their land, and its location in the global marketplace. Each country seems to feel that the land belongs to them, and has not hesitated in securing, or retaining the long term ownership of land in order to ensure that it is used to benefit the largest number of citizens for the forseeable future. In other words, land use is given pride of place in planning – particularly in respect of large infrastructure projects such as transport systems, but also in providing a good standard of housing for large numbers of people. This primary need of humans (for shelter) has not been left entirely to the market.

The shortcomings in Hong Kong are a noticeable level of inequality and a high cost of living, particularly in relation to private housing, for which it compensates in a large scheme of public housing available at low rents. Singapore on the other hand, demonstrates a slightly more equal society, which has achieved probably the highest level of owner-occupied housing in the world through a comprehensive system of planned housing development with a leasehold ownership system.

If other nations want to emulate the performance and outcomes for people living in those two societies, they would benefit from examination of the methods by which public revenue is raised, and how public infrastructure is funded. It seems to me that the key is not so much (in Hong Kong at least) the conditions of land ownership, but the methods applied to extract income from those wishing to use the land and enjoy the benefit conferred by society on particular sites.

These methods could easily be introduced in countries, even where land is owned freehold, both by changing the basis on which property taxes are levied (switching to land value rather than buildings), and by increasing the frequency of the valuations to at least annually. This should be accompanied by a shift in the burden of taxation from conventional taxes on production and consumption (income tax, national insurance and VAT for example) to unconventional taxes on rent, such as a Land Value Tax. In order to achieve economic efficiency and to optimise the use of land to create wealth, the new tax would have to have locational value at its heart, and offer no escape to those not putting the land to good use. In other words, no exemptions for undeveloped, or unoccupied bare land.

There are, of course, other economically efficient means by which public revenue could be raised. The aim should always be to ensure that the level of activity and wealth creation post tax remains the same as pre-tax. The UK affords an example: the auctioning of licences to use the 3G spectrum for mobile phones which raised £22.5bn for the public purse in April 2000.[1]

There is room for further research, and I hope this book will encourage professional economists and policy makers to pursue this to develop suitable methods ensuring a smooth transition from the current damaging tax regime to one which is more benign. However, I hope this work has also gone some way to explore an alternative model for property tenure, which would not deprive anyone of the use of land, or the fruits of their work,

---

[1] http://news.bbc.co.uk/1/hi/business/727831.stm.

as many social reformers and revolutionaries, as well as governments of the twentieth century have conspired to do.

The conundrum at the heart of this debate, is how to leave people free to use their piece of land in the way that they wish, without depriving the wider community of the benefit due to them as neighbours and creators of the effective demand that makes the occupied plot so valuable. There is a proportion of the revenue (the result of their work), which rightly belongs to the individual owner, so long as she recognises the share due to the community at large, and is willing to hand it over!

While I feel that both systems of public revenue gathering (in Hong Kong and Singapore) are superior to what we have in the UK, or anywhere else for that matter, I would not like to give the impression that everything is perfect. We have seen that there is a high degree of inequality in each country, and therefore a significant number of people either living in poverty or at least struggling to keep up with their aspirations. Each country also has its fair share of social problems, overcrowding, pollution and perhaps some of their workers suffer from high levels of stress in the race to stay ahead. Dealing with these issues is beyond the scope of this book. While the political economy can have an enormous influence on the quality of life, real progress is at least equally dependent on the philosophical and spiritual health and traditions within a country.

This analysis has concentrated very much on the practical matters of taxation and public spending, but, I hope, is nonetheless a useful pointer to a better way of arranging the affairs of humanity in other aspects.

8

Postscript

China

THROUGHOUT this book, and during my research, I have been aware of Hong Kong's rather large neighbour. I had intended to investigate the tax and land ownership arrangements in the same way as I had looked at Hong Kong, but soon recognised not only a lack of clear source material, but also a language barrier! Coupled with all of that, I have spent even less time in China than I have in Singapore or Hong Kong. I therefore abandoned that ambition for another year. Here are just a few comments and thoughts on the subject to whet your appetite.

China has historically recognised a sovereign interest in the ownership of land. Private property has not been absolute, with some kind of leasehold system in place for many centuries, so it is not surprising to find an acceptance of a concept of shared ownership/responsibility towards the land.

The first half of the twentieth century proved to be one of turmoil in China, with the demise of an Imperial Dynasty, revolution, flirtation with democracy, invasion and civil war finally leading to the establishment of a Communist dictatorship, and the division of China with the establishment of Taiwan as a separate country. Of relevance to the subject matter of this book, there were two significant factors during this period.

One, was the establishment of LVT within the German protectorate of Kiaochow (now Jiaozhou), a 400-square-mile leasehold territory on the north-eastern coast of China, arranged in 1898, and administered as a colony until 1914. Many German colonies in Africa had suffered rampant property speculation, and the authorities therefore decided to adopt Henry George's concept of a single tax based on the value of land. It was successful not only in bringing about rapid economic growth to the territory, but also financial stability. A by-product of the German presence was the founding of the Tsingtao brewery in 1903, in the city now known as Qingdao. It is probably the best known Chinese beer, and has 15% of the market in China.

The second, was the connection between Sun Yat-sen and Henry George. Dr Sun was the first President, and founding father of the Republic of China, and leader of the Kuomintang party, which although defeated in 1949, took control of Taiwan under Chiang Kai Shek. It is not clear exactly when Dr Sun read George's work, or was introduced to his ideas of the single tax, but he made frequent reference to Henry George in his writing, speeches and interviews. For example:

> I intend to devote my future to the promotion of the welfare of the Chinese people as a people. The teachings of [your] single taxer, Henry George, will be the basis of our programme of reform. The land tax as the only means of supporting the government is an infinitely just, reasonable and equitably distributed tax, and on it we will found our new system ... A single reasonable tax on the land will supply all the funds necessary to put China among the first of the civilised nations in political and economic advancement.[1]

It is likely that he would have been aware of the success of the Single Tax in Kiaochow, and in 1924 invited Dr Wilhelm Schrameier, the colonial administrator responsible for the single tax to advise on matters of administration in Canton (now Guangzhuo). The debate thereafter no doubt raged between the Nationalists, Socialists and Marxists, just as it did in Europe at the time. In China, the Communist Party eventually got the upper hand, and when they took control in 1949, the state took control of all land, both urban and rural. In rural areas, groups of households (about 160) were organised into collectives, or communes and former land owners had to give up their rights to land and join the communes. It is not clear how urban land was allocated or held by existing users after the victory of the Communists.

---

[1] *Public*, 16 (April 12th 1912) 349, reported from an interview with Sun Yat Sen in Shanghai with journalists on 4th April 1912.

As a result, China did not implement the ideas of Henry George, Dr Sun himself died in 1925, but a limited form of LVT was introduced in Taiwan after 1949, although it accounts for only a small part of the government revenue in that country today. Legal property rights for individuals were not established until the 1982 Constitution. Article 13 established rights of inheritance of property, as well as compensation for expropriation in the public interest. A more recognisable Property Law was introduced in 2007, which balanced the interests of the citizen owning property with the public interest. However, it should be made clear, these rights only refer to leaseholds or land grants, and seek to establish some basis for negotiation of compensation in cases where the state wishes to take control of the land in the public interest. There is no absolute ownership of land by individuals, and land is held on various length of lease.

Turning to taxation, probably the biggest difference in taxation method between China and the UK, is that much of the tax is collected at a regional level, showing a more or less 50/50 split between regional and national taxation. Central government sources of revenue would be fairly recognisable to UK taxpayers, including VAT, income tax, consumption tax, business tax; but a significant proportion of local government revenue is raised through land sales to developers. In the six months to June 2014, overall fiscal revenue was 7.46trn yuan, of which 3.43trn was collected by the central government, the remainder by local government. Revenue from the transfer of land use rights produced 2.11trn yuan for local government in the same period.[1] This was 28% of the total revenue, and don't forget, these transfers are not freehold sales.

For many years, land has provided both a reliable source of revenue for local government, as well as an opportunity for corruption on a grand scale owing to a lack of knowledge/understanding on the part of small farmers giving up use of the land, as well as the breakneck speed of urbanisation and development over the last thirty five years.

Each local authority at the outset of this process, seems to have made up their own rules of compensation, while individual

---

[1] news.xinhuanet.com, China's fiscal revenue growth modest, expenditure surges, 14/7/14.

officials might have enjoyed kickbacks or 'gifts' from the lucky developers securing the land for development. Most land brought into urban use had hitherto been agricultural, collectively owned land. Generally, compensation paid to the collective was based on the value of crops produced, often just six to ten times the annual yield,[1] almost always a fraction of the actual development value. Since 2013, the new premier Li has mounted a campaign against corruption, with an expensive watch on the wrist of an official often being the giveaway sign to invite further investigation. The basis for negotiating compensation has also changed, not only by implementation of new laws, but also with an awareness of the potential market price of land after development. This is now handled by Land Right Exchange Centres established in all provinces.

Urban land taken under the control of the state in 1949, could simply be allocated by local authorities for different purposes: for 'public use' such as military areas, roads, urban facilities and public services at no charge to the new user. Land could also be 'granted' for a variety of uses in city areas in return for a lump sum payment to the local authority. The term of the grant might vary according to the use – residential 70 years, manufacturing 50 years, or commercial 40 years. It is not clear whether these grants can be extended after the grant term. Leasing was introduced in the 1990s to make up for weaknesses in the grant system – the difference being, that an annual rent was agreed in place of the lump sum. Special rules apply to allocate land for use by state owned enterprises. It is not clear what the level of annual rent for such leases is, or how it is calculated.

Some have suggested that this source of revenue from land grants and lease is not sustainable, as many of the larger cities have reached the boundaries of land available for urban development.[2] In other words, China is running out of space. Cho and Choi explain in their paper, that the Government has a commitment to maintain 121.2m hectares of land in agricultural use. The current total of agricultural land is 121.7m hectares, so not much

---

[1] From Sung Chan Cho and Philip Pil Soo Choi, *Introducing Property Tax in China as an Alternative Financing Source*, Land Use Policy, Volume 38, Elsevier, 2014.

[2] *Ibid.*

more can be taken out of agricultural use, without reclaiming further land from wasteland or desert.

China has responded with the introduction of new land taxes, from 2011. These reforms to the way land is taxed, are being designed to even out the flow of revenue, and reduce the distortion and opportunity for corruption inherent in lump sum payments for land use through Land Grant or rents for a Lease. However, the impact of these new taxes is uneven across the country, and how they will fit into the overall picture remains opaque.

One unique tax in China is the so-called Land Appreciation Tax, whereby, if land (more accurately the land grant or lease) is sold to another party, progressive rates of tax are applied to the uplift in value of both land and buildings at the time of sale. The rates start at 30%, rising to 60% according to the scale of the transaction.

When I was in Hong Kong recently, I took the opportunity to spend a day in China – which is now very easy, with high speed rail lines from the centre of Hong Kong, as well as motorways running between the major cities. To take one example of a building I visited in Guangzhou: the International Finance Centre (IFC). This comprises nearly 100 floors, and combines offices, a department store, serviced apartments and five star hotel. It was developed by the Hong Kong listed Yuexiu Property Company, who paid 1.5bn rmb (£151m) for a 40-year lease on the plot. They have created 450,000 square metres of space, at a construction cost of 7bn rmb (£735m). The property was sold to a Real Estate Investment Trust for 13bn rmb (£1.3bn) on completion in 2010, and is currently valued at 30bn rmb (£3.1bn), although that is likely to fluctuate.

When I asked the Senior Finance Manager who took us round the building, about China's long term prospects, given the level of debt that has built up since the 2008 financial crash, and breakneck growth in development of both commercial and residential space, he smiled knowingly. He pointed out that the Chinese government had not sold the land for all this development, only the leases. This suggests they have an ace up their sleeve, whereby the ongoing economic activity taking place in all these buildings would eventually be tapped to help pay down the debts.

Since the financial crisis in 2008, China has avoided recession. Many people argue that this has only been possible due to a massive injection of credit for large infrastructure projects, including public transport systems, dams and roads, as well as investment in building projects up and down the country. Many of the buildings remain empty, and investors, as well as economists, fear a major crash coming China's way. They point out that much of the investment has been channeled through State Owned Enterprises (SOEs) and that the credit has been created by state owned banks. There is a fear of default on a scale not seen since 2008. I would suggest there is one major difference, which relates to the long term prospects for a country which retains a long term interest in their most valuable asset: the land. It is much easier to extract additional public revenue in these circumstances, especially where there is a tradition of leasehold ownership. So long as only the Economic Rent is collected in this way, the economic activity generating the Rent will continue as before, unaffected by the imposition of otherwise inefficient taxes. This revenue can then be used to pay down debt.

The Chinese government perhaps stands at a fork in the road in respect of how it might raise revenue in the future. One fork would take it down the western model of further taxation on production and consumption (employment, or income taxes as well as sales taxes such as VAT or GST). This would lead to the sort of problem experienced by most western economies: boom bust cycles, low growth, high taxation etc. Alternatively, the government could follow the path taken perhaps accidentally in Hong Kong, of Government Rents on the locational value of land. In my opinion this would lead to a more stable and sustainable growth rate, coupled with lower land values, and an incentive to fully exploit the economic potential of all land.

Russia faced a similar choice in 1990, after the collapse of the Soviet Union. In fact 30 American Economists, including three Nobel laureates wrote an open letter to then President Mikhail Gorbachev urging him to adopt a policy of retaining ultimate ownership of all land in order to facilitate the collection of rent. After praising Russia's intention to introduce a free market economy, they wrote:

But there is a danger that you will adopt features of our economies that keep us from being as prosperous as we might be. In particular, there is a danger that you may follow us in allowing most of the rent of land to be collected privately.

It is important that the rent of land be retained as a source of government revenue. While the governments of developed nations with market economies collect some of the rent of land in taxes, they do not collect nearly as much as they could, and they therefore make unnecessarily great use of taxes that impede their economies – taxes on such things as income, sales and the value of capital.

Users of land should not be allowed to acquire rights of indefinite duration for single payments. For efficiency, for adequate revenue and for justice, every user of land should be required to make an annual payment to the local government, equal to the current rental value of the land that he or she prevents others from using.[1]

Sadly, Gorbachev did not heed the advice, and the age of the Russian Oligarch, with its flip side of low growth and continuing poverty, was unleashed.

Taking this proven path of economic efficiency would leave China with no debt, high growth and low taxes, a combination that would prove unstoppable in the global race for economic domination. It might even force America, and other western nations to look again at the ideas and recommendations of Henry George.

---

[1] *Now the Synthesis, Capitalism Socialism & the New Social Contract*. Ed. Richard Noyes. Appendix Shepheard Walwyn 1991

Index

Andrew Purves grew up on the island of Hong Kong. He went to school in Edinburgh, and studied Modern History and Politics at London University in the early '80s. Upon graduating he went into the furniture business, working for Habitat and Liberty of Regent Street. Now with his own business in London, he is keenly aware of the less favourable economic climate in the UK which he attributes to the damaging impact the UK tax regime has on economic activity. In his spare time he teaches Economics at the School of Economic Science in London.

OUR LAND, OUR RENT, OUR JOBS

Uncovering the explosive potential for growth via resource rentals

'Lateral ideas on tax raising to generate social justice for all South Africans whilst maintaining international investor confidence' **Peter Hain**

South Africa, like many countries in Africa, is resource rich but the benefits are not shared by the whole population. High levels of unemployment are leading to increasing conflict and violence, undermining the brighter future hoped for when apartheid was abolished.

The authors set out a proposal to unleash their country's potential for growth in a way that benefits investors and the poorest by reforming taxation — a blueprint for other developing countries. The rapid development of Taiwan and South Korea in the 1950s and 1960s owed much to a similar, business-friendly tax reform.

Governments today tax social ills like tobacco and alcohol to discourage use, but do we want to discourage work and investment? The result, the authors reveal, is to make half the country economically unviable, yet economists have long known that there is a tax that does not have this adverse effect. As Adam Smith put it: 'Though a part of this revenue should be taken ... in order to defray the expenses of the state, no discouragement will thereby be given to any sort of industry.'

'... abounds with new ideas ... they must be debated, for only in this manner can a solution to the [land] crisis be found.'

Dr Thami Mazwai, University of Johannesburg

'Given the challenges of finding an equitable and efficient system for raising revenue, their proposals cause us to think creatively "out of the box" ... also a refreshing look at how South Africa's pressing problems of job creation, rapid economic growth, revenue shortfalls, corruption, and poverty can be alleviated.'

Kennedy Maxwell, past President, Chamber of Mines of South Africa

256pp   ISBN 978-0-85683-504-9   £19.95 pb